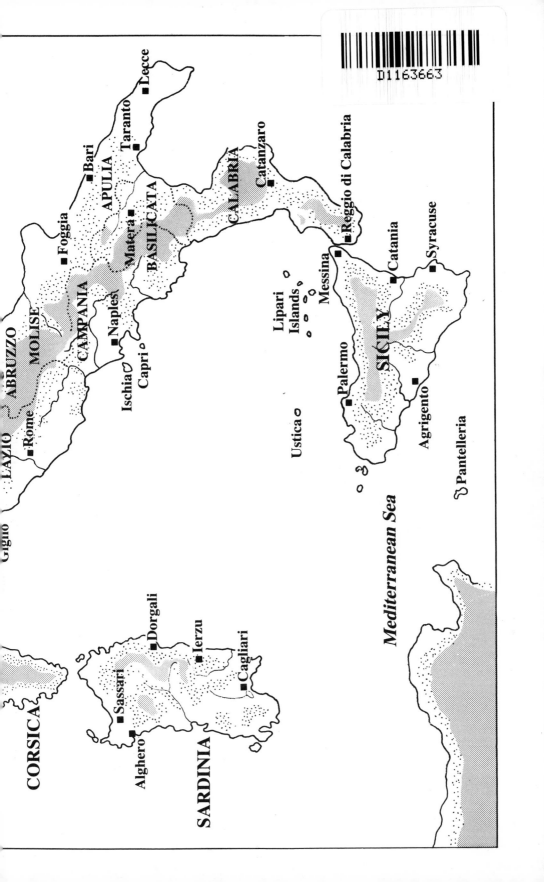

CORSICA

SARDINIA

Alghero ■

■ Sassari

■ Dorgali

■ Ierzu

Cagliari ■

Giglio

LAZIO

■ Rome

ABRUZZO

MOLISE

CAMPANIA

■ Foggia

Ischia ○

Capri ○

■ Naples

APULIA

Bari ■

Taranto

■ Lecce

BASILICATA

Matera ■

CALABRIA

Catanzaro ■

Reggio di Calabria ■■

Messina ■

Lipari
Islands ○

Ustica ○

SICILY

Palermo ■

Catania ■

Syracuse ■

Agrigento ■

Pantelleria

Mediterranean Sea

THE NEW BOOK OF

Italian Wines

By the same author

THE NEW BOOK OF
Italian Wines

Cyril Ray

SIDGWICK & JACKSON

LONDON

First published in Great Britain in 1982 by
Sidgwick and Jackson Limited

Endpaper maps by Robyn Fairweather

The publishers would like to thank
the Italian Institute of Foreign Trade
for supplying all the illustrations
(between pages 64 and 65)

ISBN 0-283-98745-6

Photoset by Robcroft Ltd, London WC1
Printed in Great Britain by
The Garden City Press Limited
Letchworth, Hertfordshire
for Sidgwick and Jackson Limited
1 Tavistock Chambers, Bloomsbury Way
London WC1A 2SG

Dedicated to the people of Italy, all of whom I love, and especially, because I love them especially, to
Colonel Luigi – 'Gigi' – Caligaris
and his wife Paola

Contents

– Sicily, Sardinia, and the Mezzogiorno – and where the changes brought about by the Italian wine law and entry into the E.E.C. had been most marked.

In addition, of course, there have been far greater opportunities than there were fifteen years ago to taste here in England virtually every important Italian wine, thanks largely to the efforts of the Institute of Foreign Trade's representatives here in London, and the enormous increase in exports to the United Kingdom (from just over 3 per cent of the total imports of wine in 1970 to nearly 17 per cent in 1980).*

I have been helped more than I can say in home-based tastings by Rosemary George, M.W., and by the following firms who have sent her and me tasting samples or arranged tasting sessions:

ASHLYNS-TRESTINI, London S.E.1.
CHRISTOPHER AND CO., LTD, London S.W.1.
GIORDANO LTD, London W.1.
HUNT AND BRAITHWAITE, London N.W.6.
MORGAN, FURZE AND CO., London W.1.
STONEHAVEN WINES, Headley Down, Hants.

I am also indebted to Miss George for helping me to unravel some of the complexities of the wine law, and for expanding what was originally an inadequate glossary. She is not only a Master of Wine but a mistress of the Italian tongue – how sad that she prefers Chablis to Soave . . .

My indebtedness to the Italian Institute of Foreign Trade, both in Rome and in London, must already be apparent, but it has become impossible for me to name all those in Italy who have smoothed my path, opening their bottles and, being Italian, their homes and their hearts to me. It took a page and a half of my earlier book to list those who had done so in the past; now they would have to be listed again, and as many more, and some names might still, by mischance, be omitted. All I can do here is to thank all the Italians who have helped me over the past forty years to learn about, and to love, the wines of Italy: in learning to love Italy and the Italians I have needed no help.

One chapter is an exception to my statement that this is an entirely new book. Chapter 2, 'A Long Look Back', is reprinted from the book published in 1966† because it is purely historical: the facts of

---

* (Excluding sparkling wines.) It must also be remembered that between 1970 and 1980 total import of wine increased by about 190 per cent. So Italy's share increased from 3 to 17 per cent of a total three times bigger than before.
† Reprinted by kind permission of the Rainbird Publishing Group Ltd.

history from the ninth century B.C. to the nineteenth century A.D. have not changed between 1964, when I wrote it, and 1981, when I write these words. Nor has my interpretation of them; and, as I wrote that brief account as well as I knew how, I could not now re-write it for the sake of a new book save for the worse. I am sure that my readers will understand and forgive: even my publisher has . . .

CYRIL RAY

Albany, London 1981

Chapter 1

The Land of Vines

ITALY is only a little larger in area than Great Britain and Ireland, three-fifths the size of France, and something like half its area is too mountainous to cultivate. Yet more wine is grown in the few thousand square miles of Italy's cultivable land than in any other country – about one-fifth of the world's wine.

The ancient Greeks, landing and settling in what became Magna Graecia – Sicily and southern Italy – called it *oenotria*, 'the land of vines', and it is even more a land of vines now than it was two and a half thousand years ago, during which time grape-growing and wine-making have spread throughout the long leg of land that is Italy.

French-speaking Italians grow wine in the Valle d'Aosta, which is farther north than France's own claret-growing vineyards; farther north still, in the latitude of Burgundy, on the lower Alpine slopes of the Alto Adige, German-speaking Italians grow wines to which they give names as German as their own; there are vineyards along the frontier with Yugoslavia tended by Italian wine-growers with Slav surnames and Slovenian accents. Sicilian wines are grown in the same latitude as the retsina of Attica and, in the island of Pantelleria, half-way to Africa. In the Alpine north, vines grow at a couple of thousand feet and more above sea-level; there are Sardinian wines from sandy soil at the edge of the sea.

So many different regions and, until recently, far too many wines with different names. In the book I published some sixteen years ago I listed six hundred or so different wines and quoted the complaint of one Italian writer, Paolo Monelli, about the omissions from the more than seven hundred listed in Luigi Veronelli's classic *I Vini d'Italia*.

At that time, only two volumes had as yet been published of the Ministry of Agriculture's *Principali Vitigni da Vino Coltivati in*

Italia; now it is complete, in five volumes, and its index runs into the thousands. Burton Anderson states that although, in a recent three-volume reference book, Gianni Bonacina listed 3,811 'more or less individually identified wines . . . even he missed some'. Mr Anderson himself lists just under six hundred in a tightly packed book of nearly as many pages. At the time of writing, there are just over two hundred D.O.C. wines and certainly no more than twice that number that have an identifiable individuality, a local habitation and a name; are reasonably available and worth looking for. Mr Anderson is about right, and I hope that I am, too: certainly some few of the six hundred I listed sixteen years ago no longer exist. The three thousand more in Signor Bonacina's three volumes, and those that he is said to have missed, must have been sub-divisions of sub-divisions – for example, there is one *denominazione* for Oltrepò Pavese, but ten Oltrepò Pavese wines, each named after its grape.

The gradual application of the Italian wine law and the more recent E.E.C. regulations have helped to tidy things up for all practical purposes, as they have in Germany, where somewhere between twenty thousand and fifty-two thousand different vineyard names (as we have already observed, it depends how you count them) were reduced at a stroke to three thousand.

The number of named *wines* is, of course, much smaller than the number of named vineyards. Some inconsiderable wine-growing districts have merged with their neighbours or disappeared altogether, and in a book for the general reader, as distinct from an encyclopaedia, the writer may reasonably overlook the sort of local wine that is available only in the local *trattoria*, owned by the grower's brother-in-law.

The committee of the Italian Ministry of Agriculture and Forests charged with according *denominazioni* did, indeed, start off on the wrong foot. Three of the first eight such distinctions awarded, in May 1966, were numbers three, four and five, to Ischia *bianco*, Ischia *rosso*, and Ischia *bianco superiore*, one apiece, which is as if the French Institut National des Appellations d'Origine were to allow separate *appellations* to Bordeaux *rouge* and Bordeaux *blanc*, Beaune *rouge* and Beaune *blanc*, and so on through the regions, so vastly increasing the number of *appellations*. (There is always a separate *appellation*, though, in France for a *supérieure*, which indicates a higher degree of alcohol.) Fortunately, representations were made so that there is now only one Ischia *denominazione* to cover all three wines, and one is now the rule, as in France, for any D.O.C. district that produces red, white and pink.

14

But in the directories and encyclopaedias, as distinct from the D.O.C. list and books such as this, and Mr Anderson's, for the general reader, there can be sixty-seven entries under Moscato alone: it is as though the French accorded separate *appellations* for the Gamay in every commune of the Beaujolais, or for the Riesling in every village of Alsace.

Although, as I have pointed out, there are more names of Italian wines than there are identifiably individual wines, nevertheless the country that produces more wine than any other also produces a range of wines varying widely in style, character and, indeed, quality and consistency. This must necessarily be so in a wine-growing country with so many different grape varieties, so many different sorts of soil – sandy and volcanic, clay, chalk and mountain slate; so many micro-climates; so many sub-cultures and so many variations, from the Alps to Etna, in local traditions and taste.

Yet I like to think – even if this is no more than a fond fancy – that the wines of Italy share a sort of family resemblance, however slight; that there is a common quality of *italianità*, Italianateness, about all Italian wines, just as there is about all Italian people – though there are far too many occasions when Torinesi and Napolitani, Veneziani, Siciliani and Sardi would still hotly dispute this. (It came as a surprise, not long before writing these words, to hear a senior Italian soldier – a Piedmontese, as are and have been so many Italian soldiers – say, 'No, old as my family is, I don't call myself, or consider myself, a Piedmontese any more: I'm an Italian, and I wish that many of my own people, and Venetians and Romans and Tuscans, felt the same.')

A diminution of self-conscious regional diversities and prejudices in the regions of Italy might be something of a disappointment to foreign visitors, but the Piedmontese brigadier was right: it would be better for Italy.

Meanwhile, I think of Italy as one when I suggest that just as the Italian language and the Italian people and the cities and villages and countryside of Italy are easy to love, so the quality common to all Italian wines, from the Merlots of the north to the Montepulcianos of the south, is that they are easy to drink.

It is generally held that the best Italian wines are less subtle than those of France – than the great clarets and white burgundies, say. I would not dispute this as a generalization, though I might suggest exceptions. But this is not necessarily to disparage the wines of Italy. Italian wine, in general, is comparable to French wine in much the same way as the cuisines of the two countries are comparable. It has been well said that if you want one great memorable meal – a work of art to remember all your life – then you must go to one of the French Michelin-three-starred temples of gastronomy, or be lucky enough to be entertained in one of the few great private houses where the same kind of chef is employed, but that if you want the sort of meal that you can eat twice a day, seven days a week, without ever being bored or dyspeptic, then the fresh food, freshly cooked, to be found in modest eating-places and private houses all over Italy is your answer. An Italian friend once put it another way: 'We eat food; the French eat sauces.' Unfair, of course, but I could see what he meant.

Yet there are great wines among those of Italy. It may be that a fine *riserva* Chianti shows less finesse than an old claret, but it makes a noble accompaniment to the lordly beefsteaks of Florence – a Brunello di Montalcino perhaps even more so. The true, dry Lambrusco of Emilia-Romagna – not the cheap, sweetish 'Lambruscola' so popular in the United States – is an ideal wine to 'cut' such rich dishes as the stuffed pig's foot, *zampone*, of Modena and Bologna. The lake district of northern Italy is picnic country, and the light red wines of the region, Bardolino and Valpolicella, are just the wines for al fresco meals by the lakeside, as are the white Soave and Verdicchio for the fish-fries of Venice and the Adriatic coast.

There are hearty reds to drink with the game of the Abruzzi and Sardinia, and one can smell the fragrance of the grape in the after-dinner Aleaticos of the south and in the lightly sparkling, uncloyingly sweet Asti Spumante, than which nothing is more delicious with a peach or a fig or an apricot, fresh from a tree that overhangs the vineyard.

All these are straightforward wines, easy to understand and to enjoy: if they wear their hearts on their sleeves, as is said of the Italian people themselves, that is no bad thing – the wines, like the people, are eager to be liked.

It used to be said that Italian wines were carelessly made and inconsistent in quality. Later chapters will show, I hope, how the Italian wine law and E.E.C. regulations have helped to give them a new status and, some of them, a new self-respect, and how the government money made available to the co-operatives of Sicily, Sardinia and the south have vastly improved both viticulture and vinification. There has been what was described recently as 'an explosive growth' in the export of Italian wine: the law and government aid have helped; so have the efforts of the Institute of Foreign Trade, Italian wine-growers, and British importers. But it is largely, too, because wine-drinkers outside Italy have learned to know, to like, and now, at last and with good reason, to trust them.

Chapter 2

A Long Look Back

THERE was wine in Italy before there was Rome. It is still a matter of scholarly debate whether the Bronze Age inhabitants of northern Italy made wine from the wild grape-vine which is known (from the grape pips found where their lake dwellings used to be) to have flourished in their time, but it is as certain as can be that the Etruscans were making and drinking wine in the regions we know now as Tuscany and Lazio in the ninth and tenth centuries B.C. (The traditional date for the founding of Rome is 753 B.C.) It is generally agreed, except by Warner Allen, that the Etruscans, 'in the days of their glory', as Charles Seltman put it, 'must have made fine drink after the manner of the Greeks and the inhabitants of Anatolia whence this remarkable people had come to settle in Italy' (in about 800 B.C.). And William Younger also held that 'they would certainly have known about viticulture in the ninth century and . . . would certainly not have been content to lead a life without wine'. They even paid their devotions to a wine god of their own, Fufluns.

Warner Allen, in his *A History of Wine*, stated that 'the Etruscans seem never to have mastered the art of viticulture', but he seems to be alone in this belief. It would be fairer to say that the Etruscans, though not by any means completely ignorant of viticulture, were amateurs at it – drinkers of immature wine from unpruned vines – compared with the Greeks, who founded a colony at Cumae, on a promontory near what is now Naples, in about 750 B.C., bringing with them 'a tried system of viticulture as well as cuttings of their vines and, equally valuable, the art of pottery, which made it possible for wine, favoured by a good year, well-made from fine grapes and stored in an air-tight earthenware receptacle, to ripen into something very different from the best wine then known in Italy'.

Not long after, it is interesting to note, other Greeks, from Ionia, founded Marseilles, and the art and science of viticulture began to spread along the valleys of the Rhône and, perhaps, the Rhine.

The Greeks of Cumae conquered the Etruscans, and the Sabines conquered the Greeks. By that time, about 420 B.C., the region around Cumae – Campania – was already famous for its wines, and Father Sabinus, the legendary founder of the Sabines, who had appropriated to themselves the culture of the conquered, eventually makes his appearance in Virgil as the Vine-Grower, with his pruning knife. All the same, the Romans of the time seem to have imported their fine wines direct from Greece, rather than to have drunk the wines grown in Campania from Greek vines in the Greek way, and to have gone on doing so well into the period when, with the conquest of Greece and the fall of Carthage, Rome became the mistress of the Mediterranean world.

Pliny, in his *Natural History*, writing in about A.D. 70, gives a curiously precise date – 154 B.C. – as the year in which Italy became the greatest wine-growing country in the world, producing about two-thirds of the eighty known varieties of fine wine. Even then, Greek wines were competing with native growths on the Roman market, and still enjoyed such prestige that that great gourmet, Lucullus, a couple of generations earlier than Pliny, distributing Greek wine to the Roman people on his return in triumph from his campaigns in the East, flattered himself on his own open-handedness – for he recalled that in his father's time guests at public banquets received only one cup of Greek wine apiece: they then had to continue with Italian wines. But by this time Falernian from Campania seems to have been prized as highly as the wines of Chios and Lesbos, and in his third consulship Caesar, in addition to Chian and Lesbian, offered not only the now famous Falernian of Campania but Mamertine from Sicily as well.

In his immense, and immensely learned, history of wine and wine-drinking, William Younger listed eighteen wines regarded by the Romans of the golden age – the latter years of the Republic and the earliest of the Empire – as being the finest in the world. Three were Greek, and all three came from the farthest of the Greek islands – Cos, Chios and Lesbos. At one time, the Greeks used to treat their wines with sea-water, as the Greeks of our own time treat theirs with resin, but the resinated wine that Rome knew, and that Martial inveighed against, came not from Greece but from northern Italy. Greece took to it later. Younger's belief, following Pliny, is that it was only as this practice of sea-watering declined that the Chian, Lesbian and Coan wines became fashionable in Rome. It is clear, however, that even before they became fashionable, they had been popular when heavily salted, and enough Romans were fond of them for Cato, in his *De Agri Cultura*, to give more than one recipe for counterfeiting Coan wine, all of them involving the addition of brine or sea-water.

There are also four Spanish wines in Younger's list, but it is the eleven Italian wines that concern us here. One was Sicilian – the Mamertine already mentioned, from around Messina, which Julius Caesar made fashionable; the remaining ten came from the mainland. Most famous of all was – and is, thanks to the frequency with which the classical writers referred to it – Falernian (see p.105), which came from the hills forming the boundary between Latium and Campania, near where Mondragone now stands. Like so many modern Italian wines with a single name, there were a dry and a sweet, a red and a white, but Warner Allen was sure that the great classic was the dry red Falernian, 'probably not unlike such a Rhône wine as Châteauneuf du Pape', but with a much more powerful bouquet (though Henderson thought it must be like a sherry or madeira), and he quotes Martial, who 'wanted not merely to drink the kisses left in the loved one's cup but to kiss lips moist with old Falernian'. Again, like so many Italian red wines of our own time, Falernian seems to have had a remarkable capacity for ageing, probably in glass or earthenware jars, sealed with a sort of plaster of Paris; Petronius, in Nero's time, makes the nouveau-riche Trimalchio serve his guests with the most expensive wine obtainable in Rome – Falernian, a hundred years old.

Similarly, Surrentine, from the Sorrentine peninsula, was said to need at least twenty-five years to lose its youthful asperity. It takes its place among Younger's pre-eminent eighteen wines largely, it seems, because of its reputation in classical times as a tonic, much prescribed by the physicians; two Roman emperors in succession, Tiberius and Caligula, found it too thin for their tastes – Caligula, indeed, scorned it as *nobilis vappa*.*

Calenian, a lighter wine than Falernian, but from the same parts (near the present-day Calvi), is mentioned time and again in Horace – though Horace admits that he offers it to Maecenas only because he cannot afford Falernian; and so is the dry, full-flavoured

---

* Badly kept wine turns to vinegar, and the Latin word for vinegar that had in its turn become insipid was *vappa*. The Emperor considered Surrentine to be flavourless vinegar with ideas above its station. By extension, the word *vappa* came to be used for a stupid good-for-nothing; it persists as *voppo* in Neapolitan slang, and entered the American vocabulary by way of immigrants from the south, becoming 'wop' in the process – all this according to Charles Seltman in his *Wine in the Ancient World*.

Caecuban, which before the time of Augustus was tremendously fashionable, though it must have been a coarse, heavy and headachey wine (Henderson believed it to be a rough sweet wine), from vines trained up the poplars that grew in the marshes between Terracina and Formiae. As Warner Allen observed, vines grown in a marsh can never produce really fine wines, and Cyrus Redding went further, stating that 'soil infected by stagnant waters' is the only ground in which the vine will not grow. In any case Caecuban ceased to be produced when Nero drove the Baiae-Ostia canal through its native swamps.

Setine must have been finer: it came from notably beautiful vineyards overlooking the Pontine marshes, and was thought by some of his courtiers to be Augustus's favourite wine – which meant, of course, that it became theirs. Others claimed that distinction for the north-Italian Rhaetic, which must have pleased Virgil, for it came from the hills above Verona, near his birthplace, Mantua, and he loved it dearly. The Sicilian Mamertine and Rhaetic are the only Italian wines among the eighteen not from either Campania or Latium; Rhaetic is the exception to the general opinion of the time that no wine worth drinking came from north of Rome. Opinion in modern times is all the other way. Rhaetic came, in any case, from just about the same region as the Soave of our own time, and may perhaps have been a similar wine – we know it to have been light and delicate, a pleasant change for Augustus from the heavy wines of Latium and Campania, the admirers of which found it mawkish.

Of the remaining wines, Alban was the precursor of the present-day *castelli Romani* wines, coming from the Alban Hills: there were a sweet and a dry, both perhaps white. Massic came from the same area as Falernian and Calenian, which it resembled, and Fundanian was very similar to the heavy Caecuban; Statanian came from the fringe of the Falernian country and was lighter than most.

'In ancient times,' wrote Cyrus Redding more than a century ago, 'the Romans trained their high vines as they now do in Tuscany, along palisades, or from tree to tree.' In Tuscany, this pattern has only recently changed and many vines in central and south-central Italy are still trained in this way, so that the twentieth-century holiday-maker, on his way to Florence or Siena, Verona or Bologna, can see how Horace's Calenian, or Virgil's Rhaetic, was grown, using the system known to the Romans as the *arbustum*.

A variation of this method was the *compluvium*, a rectangular trellis raised above the ground, forming a sort of arbour – still a 'high vine' system, and with the same advantage as the *arbustum*, in that either under the trees or over the trellises the vines could be trained in such a way as to be shielded by foliage from too great a measure of sunshine.

The vines of southern Italy, on the other hand, were trained low, using the system now known as *albarello*, perhaps brought in by the Greeks. This was an easier and cheaper method, for it obviates the expense of trees or trellises, and much of the trouble of training, but it produces coarse wines because of the reflection of heat from the soil, and in Roman times was said to encourage the depredations of foxes, rats and mice. This system is only now slowly dying out in the south.

Cellaring must have been well understood by the Romans, even though they seem to have kept their wines above ground, in what the French would call *chais* rather than *caves*. Various writers, Henderson points out, ' . . . generally advise a northern aspect, and one not much exposed to the light, in order that it may not be liable to sudden vicissitudes of temperature; and they very properly inculcate the necessity of placing it at a distance from the furnaces, baths, cisterns, or springs of water, stables, dunghills and every sort of moisture and effluvia likely to affect the wine.'

The better wines were matured in a *fumarium*; indeed, references in Latin authors to 'smoky' wines have suggested to some historians that the wine itself was smoked, and led to curious speculations as to what it could have tasted like. But it seems reasonable to suppose that the reference was not to a sort of kippered claret but simply to the process to which the wine had been subjected. It must therefore be thought probable that Roman wines were subjected to heat, as madeira is to this day, for the purpose both of mellowing and of stabilizing it.

From Cato, who flourished around 200 B.C., to Columella, between two and three hundred years after – as it might be from Isaac Newton to our own time – a great number of Latin authors produced treatises on agricultural methods. From them William Younger made tentative identification of some of the grapes of classical times with some of present-day Italy, notably the Aminean with the Greco Bianco and the Trebulan with the Trebbiano, both producing white wine.

Columella preferred the Aminean to the more prolific Nomentan for precisely the same reason that in Burgundy, for instance, the Pinot is a 'noble' grape and the more prolific Gamay is not. By this time (in the early years of the Empire under Claudius or Nero), wine-growing on the sizeable estates of Latium and Campania was well-informed and technically well organized – which is not to say that the greater part of Italy's wine did not come from small-holdings on which peasant farmers made rough wines from common grapes by the simplest methods, and drank them young. A wine-grower such as Columella himself took great trouble over his cuttings and graftings, picking each variety of grape individually, and laying it down that 'we judge to be best every kind of wine which can grow old without any treatment, nor should anything at all be mixed with it, which might dull its natural flavour. For that wine is immeasurably the best, which needs only its own nature to give pleasure.'*

Macaulay wrote that

> This year the must shall foam
> Round the white feet of laughing girls
> Whose sires have marched to Rome.

But that was in the time of Tarquin, which is pre-history, and there is plenty of evidence that the finer wines of classical times were pressed, not trodden, before fermentation in great earthenware jars, and that the Romans knew a great deal about fining and racking. They also devised a sort of *chaptalisation*, making use of honey or boiled must, for thin wines lacking in natural grape-sugar. Boiled must was also used to produce fortified dessert wines, as is done with *vin cotto* (see Appendix 1); some wines were preserved, or flavoured, or both, by the addition of herbs, spices, or, as in Greece, resin; and there are unappetizing recipes in Cato, Virgil, Pliny and others for cheap wines, many of them made from a second pressing, as rations for farm-workers. Pliny, indeed, writing in the first decades A.D., complained that even the nobility were fobbed off with coloured and adulterated wines.

No doubt there were genuine wines, carefully produced by wine-growers as dedicated to quality as Columella, but, as William Younger has deduced from the cookery books of the time, those Romans who were not given to country dishes and the simple life, as Horace was (or, at any rate, as Horace sang), lusted after pungency and richness, their dishes spiced and peppered, and enjoyed wines to match. Spiced and aromatic wines, or the Roman version of *retsina*, would no doubt go well with such dishes as dormice fattened on chestnuts and cooked in a sauce made of the entrails of salted Spanish mackerel and pepper. We know, too, that there were wines made specially to be drunk as aperitifs or as dessert wines, flavoured

* Warner Allen's translation.

with honey, violets, roses or pepper, as well as an absinthe (*absinthites*) made of wine and wormwood.

Most of the true, unadulterated wines, such as Falernian, were probably, as we have seen, big, full-flavoured, heavy red wines; the light, dry Rhaetic, possibly white, was one of the few exceptions – perhaps the Romans drank it with the oysters they loved so much. The Roman love for rich dishes would explain the popularity of such wines, though there are many references to their being drunk diluted with water, or with snow. There were drinking parties, and there were heavy drinkers, but the Romans generally, in the great days of the city, were an abstemious people, and to drink wine undiluted was to go it rather. Catullus sang the promise of a drinking bout with a hard-drinking companion in his *Minister vetuli puer Falerni*:

> Bearer of old Falernian wine,
> Good boy, a stronger glass be mine.
> Mistress of toasts (as drunk as she
> Not ev'n the drunken grape can be)
> Postumia will have it so.
> You, water, wine's destruction, go:
> Away with you to folk austere:
> The god of wine himself is here.*

– which suggests that Falernian was usually offered diluted and that this was a special occasion.

All the same, the great wines, even if destined for diluton were handled with some connoisseurship. They were usually decanted, strained either through linen or through metal wine-strainers that may perhaps have resembled those made by the great Georgian silversmiths.

They would have needed decanting, too, for the best and most highly prized of these big, heavy wines spent many years in cask (or, more likely, in earthenware jars, though wooden casks were not unknown), and in smaller glass or earthenware bottles, before being served. There are endless references in the classical authors, from Cato onwards, to the age of wines of the better sort – such as Horace's promise to Maecenas that a jar of mellowed wine had long been waiting for him, and Columella's assertion that almost all wine improved with age. Not that there were vintage years as such: as in Italy now, it is how many years a wine has aged in cask and bottle

---

* Macnaghten's translation.

that matters, not in what year it was made.* True, most of the wine of Italy was for immediate consumption by the farmer who grew it and his family – wine of the country that was drunk within the year. But even Horace's modest Sabine wine, which no doubt bore about the same relation to Falernian as a common Beaujolais would to a Romanée-Conti, or a Blayais to a first-growth of the Médoc, and was by no means, it would seem, a 'big' wine, was ready to drink, wrote Horace, only after from seven to fifteen years; the marsh-grown Caecuban also took many years to mature, while we have already recorded the quarter of a century that was needed to smooth away the harshness of Surrentine.

We cannot know now, for certain, what any of these wines tasted like, but it is clear, at any rate, that the best wines of classical Rome were grown, made, cellared and decanted as carefully as any first-growth claret that reaches the table of a twentieth-century connoisseur. And although much of this skill and care and devotion was forgotten, along with much else, for centuries after the fall of Rome to the barbarians, much remained. It is not so much that the arts of living were all lost in the Dark and the Middle Ages as that a great deal went unrecorded: there is a link between the vineyards that Virgil knew, in northern Italy, and the Vernage, or Vernaccia,† that came to England from those parts in the fourteenth and fifteenth centuries; and Trubidiane, recorded as having been imported into London by 1373, is a corruption of Trebbiano, which has been at any rate tentatively identified with the Trebulan that was grown in Campania in Julius Caesar's time.

We know little of Italian viticultural techniques in the Middle Ages, but Italy always remained a wine-growing country: André Simon, in his *History of the Wine Trade in England*, recorded the capture by French pirates in 1472 of a Venetian carrack bound for England with more than four hundred casks of sweet wine on board. It may well be that this particular cargo was of wines from Greece or the Levant, for Venice enjoyed the carrying trade between those

---

* Though the Romans usually knew a wine's year, and some were especially highly thought of. 'The ancients noted the years of celebrated growths, as that of the Opimian year, or the year of Rome, 632, when Opimius was consul. It was in high esteem a century afterwards. The Romans marked their amphorae, or wine vessels (containing seven gallons and a pint modern measure), with the consul's name, which indicated the year of the vintage. Many amphorae now exist with the legible mark of the vintage' (Redding). The Opimian year was 121 B.C., and it was the Opimian wine that Trimalchio offered his guests (see p.20). But it was age rather than vintage that usually impressed.
† Not to be confused with the Sardinian Vernaccia.

parts and the west and north of Europe, but that there were sweet Italian wines being carried to England at the same time is shown by the monopoly granted to the port of Southampton by Henry IV for the importation of 'Malmseys, Muscadels, and all the sweet Levant, Greek or Italian wines, imported either by foreigners or by natives'. And by the seventeenth century, 'Florence wine', white and red, meaning in fact the wine of Tuscany, is being constantly mentioned in English literature – from Lady Sandwich's present of two bottles to Pepys to take home for his wife to Salmon's complaint that although red and white Florence wines are both very good stomach wines, 'the red is something binding'. The same period sees mention of Lacryma Christi and of 'Leattica' – Aleatico – both to be found in the following pages among the familiar Italian wines of our own time.

The Florence wines were apparently exported in uncorked flasks, sealed with olive oil and packed in chests: they were very popular in England. A silver wine-label, or bottle-ticket, inscribed 'Flore', is listed in N. M. Penzer's book, where an offer in a *London Gazette* of 1707 is noted of 'A Parcel of extraordinary good Red Florence at 6s. a Gallon', and there is reference in a letter of Horace Walpole's to the British ambassador at the court of the Grand Duke of Tuscany, asking him to send Fox 'two chests of the best Florence wine every year'. A century earlier, according to Henderson, 'in the time of our own James I, to have drunk Verdea is mentioned among the boasts of a travelled gentleman.'*

It seems clear, though, that Italian wines were no longer so sturdy, or so capable of ageing, as in the days of the great Falernians. Warner Allen quotes Dean Swift's complaint, in 1711, of going to a tavern, after 'a scurvy dinner', to drink Florence 'at four-and-sixpence a flask; damned wine'. The same irascible cleric was given one of the chests that the Grand Duke of Tuscany had sent to Bolingbroke, which he 'liked mightily' at first, but which began to spoil within a fortnight, causing Swift to write to Stella: 'Do you know that I fear that my whole chest of Florence is turned sour, at least the first two were, and hardly drinkable? How plaguy unfortunate am I! And the Secretary's own is the best I ever tasted!'

There can be little doubt that Italian wines were made less carefully than in classical times and that, as William Younger wrote, there was no scientific viticulture between the fall of the Roman Empire and the agricultural innovations of the eighteenth century.

---

* Verdea is a grape variety that gave its name to what is now a little regarded Apulian wine.

Even then, technical improvements came more slowly on the Continent, and especially in Italy, than in the England of the enclosures, of Coke of Holkham and 'Turnip' Townshend. Indeed, by Cyrus Redding's time, in the 1850s, Italian wine had gone completely out of favour in England, simply because, as Redding observed in his *History and Description of Modern Wines*, 'Italian wines have stood still and remained without improvement, while those of France and Spain . . . have kept pace to a certain extent with agricultural improvement and the increasing foreign demand'.

After examining the difficulties that the wine-grower of a still disunited Italy found in the way of producing good wines for export ('trampled by the Austrian military tyranny, or by the feet of Church despots, destitute of adequate capital, and weighed down by a vexatious system of imposts, what has he to hope for by carrying towards perfection an art which can bring him no benefit?'), Redding went on:

There are places, however, where very good wine is made, and something like care bestowed upon its fabrication; but those exceptions are the result of the care of the proprietor for his own individual consumption. The curses of a foreign yoke and of domestic exaction blight the most active exertions, and render that land, which is the gem of the earth in natural gifts, a waste, or a neglected and despoiled heritage to its inhabitants. The Italians would soon make good wine, if good wine would repay the making – if they might reap that reward due to industry and improvement, which common policy would not withhold in other countries. The peasantry generally are not an idle race.

Though Redding somewhat qualifies that final tribute in going on to give another of the reasons why Italy lagged so long behind France in producing wines worthy of her soil and her long tradition: 'A fine climate, to which the wine seems wedded, produces a large quantity of rich fruit with little trouble, and why should the peasant not enjoy, without extra care and labour, that which, on his bestowing care and labour, will yield him no additional benefit?'

Even while Redding was revising his book, though, there were reforms on foot in the Chianti country.* He admitted himself that:

. . . in Tuscany, indeed, things have been at times somewhat

---

* Redding's classic work first appeared in 1833. The third edition, added to and revised, consulted for this present book, appeared in 1860.

better. . . . In particular districts in Italy it is by no means a rare thing to meet with good wine. The general neglect of a careful and just system of culture, and the want of that excitement that interest creates, have not prevented the capabilities of the Italian vineyards from being known. In certain instances much care is bestowed upon the vine. In spots among the Apennines the vines are carefully dressed, terrace-fashion, and were they well pruned, and the fruit taken in due maturity, and regularly assorted, which it rarely or never is, a vast deal of excellent wine might be made, without altering anything essential besides, in the present system of vine husbandry. There is good-bodied wine to be produced in Naples for twopence-halfpenny English a bottle, and at Rome and Florence for fourpence.

The Austrian military tyranny, the temporal despotism of the Church and the imposts between petty principalities have all long disappeared. Now, with the new wine law, the growers' associations, viticultural stations experimenting with French vines and German crosses, and new co-operative wineries, another era is dawning for Italian wines, possibly as golden as in the days when Horace, over his glass of modest Sabine, knew that he was at the centre of the wine-growing world.

Chapter 3

The Law and the Label

FROM time almost immemorial, not only in wine-growing countries but also in countries where wine is drunk but not grown, laws have been made, some effectual and many not, to protect consumers against fraud on the part of those who *sell* wine – innkeepers, vintners and others. But the regulation and control of the *growing* and *making* of wine are relatively recent, being possible only in countries with able and stable administrations, with the necessary scientific knowledge to understand what regulations need to be formulated, and an efficient bureaucratic apparatus to apply them.

From almost as soon as national unity was achieved – certainly from the 1880s onwards – successive Italian governments attempted to draft wine laws of sorts; some were actually passed, but with little serious effect. Indeed, it was not until 1963 that all such existing laws were amended and added to – some elaborated, some simplified – and gathered into a portmanteau measure. Of this important milestone in the history of Italian wine, much more later, but it must be mentioned here that, long before it was passed, a few voluntary groups of growers (*consorzi*) had been able to persuade successive governments to delimit the areas in which their wines were grown and to give their names legal protection – measures designed much more to prevent unfair competition, against what in English law is 'passing off' by unscrupulous growers and vintners, than to protect the consumer, an incidental benefit. The archetype is the *Consorzio per la Difesa del Vino Tipico del Chianti*, which secured such recognition in 1932 for its Chianti Classico (see p. 89), though this was neither the first nor the last. But these measures were too haphazard and too piecemeal ever to serve as a substitute for a national wine law.

What the law of 1963 set out to do was to establish three

controlled and protected categories of Italian wine:

Denominazione di origine semplice
(Simple denomination of origin)

Denominazione di origine controllata
(Controlled denomination of origin: D.O.C.)

Denominazione di origine controllata e garantita
(Controlled and guaranteed denomination of origin: D.O.C.G.)

Before the law came fully into effect, E.E.C. regulations, which override those of member countries, abolished the *semplice* category; at the time of writing, what are to be the first D.O.C.G. wines have already been announced: Barolo and Barbaresco from Piedmont, and Vin Nobile di Montepulciano and Brunello di Montalcino from Tuscany. Although this is now well-known, the D.O.C.G. rank will not be confirmed – the badges of rank will not be put up, so to speak – until 1985, because not until then will the Brunello di Montalcino made since the announcement have spent the requisite ageing period in wood.

It is understood that Chianti (Tuscany) and Albana di Romagna (Emilia-Romagna) will be the next D.O.C.G. wines. Chianti in particular, because of the vast production, the various styles and qualities, and the differences of opinion and of interest between growers, *consorzi* and others, will be a severe test for a system that will then include a category not only controlling methods of production and guaranteeing the integrity of place-names but also guaranteeing quality.

The abolition of the *semplice* category has led to some confusion not only among consumers but even among growers. First of all, wines not accorded a *denominazione di origine controllata* were simply *vini da tavola*, simple table wines, provided, of course, that they fulfilled the Italian government's and the E.E.C.'s basic requirements for wine meant to be sold to the consumer as such: that they must reach a minimum degree of alcohol (for Italy 9°, but not exceeding 15°), and must be made from the fermentation of the juice of fresh grapes, grown in registered vineyards.

Recently, the E.E.C. has permitted a higher category or subcategory of *vini da tavola* – *vini da tavola con indicazione geografica* – but although wines thought to be entitled to this denomination are listed by some authorities* it is not as yet,

---

* Notably in the *Guida ai Vini d'Italia*, published as recently as October 1980, one of the contributors to which is Paolo Desana, a sometime Piedmontese senator, the

according to the Agricultural Department of the Italian Institute of Foreign Trade, officially recognized – or, perhaps it is more accurate to state, it has not yet been incorporated into the Italian wine law.

In each of the following chapters on the various regions of Italy, the wines listed in the *Guida* as being *con indicazione geografica* form the basis of the list of 'other wines' that follows that of the *denominazione di origine controllata* wines of the region. The postponement of final confirmation of the D.O.C.G. ranks, and the confusion over *vini da tavola*, has left those wines with *denominazione di origine controllata* status – usually referred to in print as D.O.C. wines, and informally, by Italians in conversation, as 'dock' – as the outward and visible signs of the Italian wine law; they set the standards by which it is judged.

The first *denominazioni di origine controllata* were granted, by the special committee of the Ministry of Agriculture and Forests, in May 1966. Three years had been spent in hammering out, with regional governments and provincial council* chambers of commerce, *consorzi* of growers, and other interested parties, as well as parliamentary legal draftsmen and the like, the details of the regulations to be applied, and in soliciting, awaiting, deliberating over and deciding upon application for recognition. Like an umpire's decision on 'out' or 'not out', the *denominazione* is accorded or refused only when asked for. This is one reason – there are others, as will be seen – why some wines that certainly should have D.O.C. status are not thus distinguished: for one reason or another the growers have preferred it so.

By the middle of 1981, the official list of D.O.C. wines ran to 201 names and accounted for between 12 and 15 per cent of Italy's total production of wine. It is the stated purpose of the E.E.C. that this figure should be increased to match the proportion of French total production – 20 per cent – entitled to *appellation contrôlée* status, A.O.C. (or A.C.), the very near equivalent of D.O.C.: this figure will

driving force behind the Italian wine law of 1963, chairman of the committee that administers it, and the greatest authority on the subject.

* There are twenty regions in Italy, corresponding to former historic divisions of the country – mostly what were once independent kingdoms or grand duchies, dependencies of foreign powers or of the Pope, or combinations of such. Some, such as Sicily, Sardinia and the largely French-speaking Valle d'Aosta, have a measure of autonomy. A 'province' is a district administered by a major town or city in each region: Siena and Florence, for instance, are not only cities but provinces within the region of Tuscany. In the thinly populated Lucania (Basilicata) the only two provinces are dependent on the two towns, Potenza and Matera.

probably be reached in the near future, perhaps by the time this book is published.

The whole idea is, of course, a piece of preposterous bureaucratic nonsense. Who is to say that the proportion of total wine production reaching specific controlled standards of provenance and methods of production should be exactly the same in Italy and France? And why should they? And is every other wine-growing country in the E.E.C. – Germany, Luxembourg, Greece and, eventually, Portugal and Spain – to be obliged to follow suit?

It would be just as sensible for the Italian government to oblige every region in the country to make sure that 20 per cent of its total production was of D.O.C. standard, whereas in fact, although every one of Italy's twenty regions produces wine, the proportion of D.O.C. wines in each varies from none at all in Molise (out of forty million litres total production) and ½ of 1 per cent in Campania to 47 per cent in Trentino-Alto Adige and an average of more than 50 per cent in the Veneto, Piedmont and Tuscany.

The E.E.C. requirement is a bar to experiment and progress. Many very good wines are not eligible for D.O.C. status because they use grapes not recognized in their particular zone: the Tuscan Sassicaia, for instance (p.96), because it is made from Cabernet Sauvignon, a grape that is 'classic' in France and in some regions of Italy but not authorized for a D.O.C. Tuscan wine; and the Corvo wines of Sicily (pp.133-4) because they are blended (and to a very good standard) from grapes grown not in any one recognized zone but all over Sicily. Insistence that the country as a whole should produce a specified minimum of D.O.C. wines might not inhibit these particular producers, but might cause pressure to be brought to bear on others not to do likewise. This would stifle enterprise, and the planting of vines that in the light of modern knowledge are more suitable than those traditional to a particular zone, and thus the only ones recognized.

The Italian D.O.C. laws resemble the French A.C. laws very closely. It would take a disproportionate number of pages of this book – it would take, indeed, a whole book – to describe in detail the way a bottle of D.O.C. wine is controlled, from the pruning of the vine to the labelling of the bottle. A few instances, themselves given only in general, not in detail, must suffice:

The wine must come from a clearly and officially defined zone.

It must be made from varieties of grape recognized as having been regularly grown in that zone for at least ten years and as being varieties of a certain quality. (As in France there are 'noble' grapes, and a grape can be 'noble' in one zone but not in another – this also inhibits replanting with varieties recently found to be more suitable.)

If more than one accepted variety of grape is used, then the proportions are laid down (for example, the Barbera d'Alba of Piedmont must be made entirely of the Barbera grape; the Verdicchio dei Castelli di Jesi of the Marche must be made from the Verdicchio but with a permitted proportion of up to 15 per cent altogether of Trebbiano and Malvasia.)

Maximum yield per hectare is also laid down, so that quality is not sacrificed to quantity. Linked with this is the requirement that, each year, growers must declare their total production of the particular wine grown for D.O.C. recognition: if the specified limit is exceeded, the whole crop is declassified. This is stricter than the A.C. rule in France, where only the *surplus* is declassified.

Minimum alcohol levels are laid down: a wine's capacity for improving in cask and/or bottle and its general staying power depend to a great extent on alcoholic strength.

Chaptalisation – the addition of sugar to ferment into alcohol, thus bringing up the strength of wines otherwise too weak for their style and quality – is strictly forbidden in Italy, though it is permitted in some French wine-growing regions and allowed by request in others in bad ripening years. (To be fair to France, it must be pointed out that the need hardly arises in most parts of Italy, where there is almost invariably stronger sun in the ripening period.)

Pruning and other vineyard practices must accord with local custom.

Vinification, like varieties of grape and viticultural practice, must also conform to the traditions of the zone: at what stage, for instance, the must is taken off the skins, the period of maturing in wood, and so on.

As in France, irrigation is forbidden.

Also as in France, the grower must keep a precise record of every step in his vine-growing and wine-making, and official, authenticating documents must accompany the wine on its every move.

The regulations seem to me to be at their weakest when they lay down the 'characteristics' of a D.O.C. wine as it reaches the consumer. In a long and informative appendix on D.O.C. law to his book *Italian Wines*, Philip Dallas takes as an example the D.O.C. decree for the Umbrian Torgiano, red and white, as laid down in 1968. These particular wines are required to display the following characteristics:

33

Red Torgiano

Clarity:	Brilliant
Colour:	Ruby red
Aroma:	Vinous, delicate
Taste:	Dry, harmonious and of good body

White Torgiano

Clarity:	Brilliant
Colour:	Straw yellow
Aroma:	Vinous, light and pleasing
Taste:	Lightly fruity but pleasantly sharp

Most, if not all, of these required characteristics are a matter of subjective judgment. I have seen it nowhere explained who determines whether a certain wine meets the requirements, whether a single judge or a panel of judges, how the judges are chosen, whether they award points out of a total, and whether failure under one heading means total failure or whether it takes more than one black ball to exclude.

Such handbooks as the Paronetto *Guida*, and all guides published by regional authorities, simply give these 'characteristics' as descriptions of each wine, along with such other legal requirements as the specified grape varieties and minimum alcoholic strength. It must be made clear that they are not expert assessments of what each wine is like, but the official view of what it ought to be, confirmed by an official decision that it conforms. It accounts for the boring sameness about the notes on each of Italy's couple of hundred D.O.C. wines in official publications and in books by individual non-official authors who copy them.

Only to a very limited extent do these 'characteristics' indicate – still less do they guarantee – quality, save to the extent to which truth to its origins is in itself a quality in a wine. But if D.O.C. guaranteed quality in its fullest sense there would be no need for a D.O.C.G. category, for which there will be stricter quality control and compulsory estate bottling. As I have written elsewhere about the French A.C. and V.D.Q.S.* *appellations*, what D.O.C. guarantees, even with its 'characteristics' (and the French, being a precise and logical people, have no truck with such vague considerations), is that the wine concerned comes from where it says it does; is made in the prescribed way, traditional in and suitable to its particular region; and is made of the proper, prescribed grapes, pruned and

* The French A.C. *appellation* is virtually identical with D.O.C. There is no Italian equivalent – yet, at any rate – to the lower V.D.Q.S.

tended in the appropriate way, grown in suitable soil, and not in such a way as to sacrifice quality to quantity. Some years' wines will be better than those of other years – the D.O.C. committee can control wine-growers and wine-makers but not the weather, nor the skill and dedication of the individual producer, nor the way that casks and bottles are cared for in shippers' warehouses and wine-merchants' cellars, or on the shelves of supermarkets.

Up to that point, though, control of D.O.C. wines is both detailed and rigid, to an extent that would make a British farmer forget his grumbles about boards and ministries, look upon the forms he has to fill in for the tax-gatherer as so much child's play, and confine his wails of woe to the weather.

The producers of D.O.C. wines value their *denominazioni* all the same: D.O.C. wines pay no E.E.C. levy or compensatory tax on their export, as do non-D.O.C.; only D.O.C. wines are given special prominence abroad by the Italian Institute for Foreign Trade, a government body, in foreign markets, where they are accorded greater prestige and command higher prices. Partly for this very reason, and partly because they are virtually the only Italian wines that the enquiring amateur or the British writer about wine can discover anything about, they are usually the only wines described in official regional publications.

It is important to note that there is a more general E.E.C. wine category, V.Q.P.R.D. – *vin de qualité produit en régions déterminées*, or 'quality wine produced in specific regions'. French A.C. wines and Italian D.O.C. and D.O.C.G. wines come as of right into this category, and so eventually will Italian *vini da tavola con indicazione geografica* (or *vini tipici*), when this category is formally incorporated into the Italian wine law. French V.D.Q.S. wines (*vins délimités de qualité supérieure*) already qualify, but the possibility of confusion between the V.Q.P.R.D. of the E.E.C. and the V.D.Q.S. of the French wine law is obvious, and it is equally obvious why the initials V.Q.P.R.D. do not appear on the labels of French A.C. and Italian D.O.C. wines: they are both a cut above the French V.D.Q.S. category, and would not wish to appear to have been down-graded.

What, then, of the non-D.O.C. wines? As I have already explained, some producers, such as those of Sassicaia and the Corvo wines, which might well be up to D.O.C.G. standard if they wished, or if regulations permitted, are not in the D.O.C. list. They would be in the *semplice* category, if it still existed, but as matters stand at present they would probably – the Corvo wines certainly – be excluded even from the category of *vini da tavola con indicazione geografica* when it becomes a part of the Italian wine law.

It would seem that, at the time of writing, what is not D.O.C., unless it is simply wine sold straight from the cask at the cellar-door, is *vino da tavola*, similar to the French *vin de table* and the German *Deutscher Tafelwein*, but rather more precisely defined, because its label must indicate variety of grape, colour and place of origin. Eventually, many of these wines – pretty well all those, I imagine, sold or known at all outside their own immediate district – will qualify as *vini da tavola con indicazione geografica* or, the same thing, as *vini tipici*.

There is no Italian equivalent to the ordinary German *Tafelwein*, without the *'Deutscher'*. A *Tafelwein*, simply, may be a blend of German wine with that of any other E.E.C. country (blended with wine from non-E.E.C. countries, it is not considered even as *Tafelwein*). Italy's wine production is such that the importation of foreign wines to stretch Italian wine is unthinkable. Italy's only wine imports are of *de luxe* wines in bottle, such as champagne and first-growth clarets, for *de luxe* hotels and the tables of the rich, and of wines that she does not grow herself – port, sherry and the like, and not much of those.

Indeed, Italy's immense production is the cause of the disturbances in the South of France, where wine-growers have been demonstrating, sometimes violently, against the importing of cheap Italian wine, most of it from the Mezzogiorno, and especially from Sicily and Sardinia, which big French importers bottling brand-name wines for the supermarket trade want to blend with the thinner, paler wine from southern French vineyards, to deepen colour and flavour and increase alcoholic strength (which determines price). The difficulties are intensified by the fact that improved techniques have increased yields both in southern Italy and in the almost as prolific vineyards of France's own deep south – especially in Languedoc-Roussillon – just at a time when consumption in these two biggest wine-producing countries in the world is in decline.

In August 1981 the *Sunday Times* reported that not only have French growers been overturning Italian wine-tank lorries and boarding Italian ships in the port of Sète to spill or foul the wine they carry, but that customs officials are supporting their campaign by taking advantage of the E.E.C. rule that wine import documents must state the country of origin by impounding Italian wines that give Sicily or Sardinia instead of Italy as the producing country. At the time of writing, this particular ploy seems unlikely to be allowed to continue, but it illustrates the problem.

It would seem to the disinterested outsider that the French

growers would do better do vent their spleen upon their own big-business fellow-countrymen rather than upon Italian growers who, like themselves, are doing their job of growing wine and trying to make an honest living out of it, within the law. But who should vent his spleen upon the German firms that import cheap Italian white wine, blend it with the cheapest German, and perhaps not very much of that, and put it up in hock or (less usually) in Moselle bottles, with labels depicting Rhine castles and dimpled, dirndled fräuleins, and German names in Gothic lettering? Shippers in Britain of Italian wines are indignant, as well the duped British consumer might be. (I do not suppose that much of the stuff is sold in Germany or that French wine-drinkers are interested in German-looking wines, but the law permits the blending, so long as the wine makes no claim on its label to be *Deutscher Tafelwein*. It is sold under brand-names and, so long as it is wholesome, no law is broken.) It can be argued that at any rate Italian wine-growers and exporters have made their money out of it, and against the British consumer that if he likes the wine (or the price) he has no cause to complain. But even if the wine leaves no nasty taste in the mouth, the intent to deceive does, and in the long run it is the reputation of the German wine trade that suffers.

What concerns us here, though, is what is required of an Italian bottle and label. Eventually, the bottle capacity will be standardized at 75cl., with halves, quarters, and magnums in multiples or fractions of that or of one litre. It takes so long for bottle factories to be rejigged and for present stocks to be exhausted, however, that other sizes – notably the 72cl. traditional in many parts of Italy – will be permitted until the end of 1988.

Meanwhile, the letter 'e' may be used to show that the appropriate E.E.C. regulation is already being observed, but this is optional. Rare old bottles of great wines still in cellars will not, of course, be affected.

It is only the Italian wine law at present that requires alcoholic strength to be shown, but there is a move for it to become an E.E.C. obligation – possibly by the end of 1982, but with a long period of grace. Wherever possible, I have shown such strengths in this book; such figures are not regarded in the United Kingdom as being of especial importance or interest, but they are useful in indicating relative strengths between otherwise similar wines. In assessing them the English reader will be helped by bearing in mind that claret is usually rather more than 10°, Sauternes rather more than 13° and Châteauneuf du Pape rather more than 12·5° (these are the minima required for the wines to qualify for *appellations*), and that 14° is the point above which the British Customs and Excise exact the higher duty levied on fortified as distinct from 'light' wines.

The explanation of how the alcoholic strength figure is arrived at I take – gratefully, because I can neither understand nor explain it myself – from Bruno Roncarati's *Viva Vino*:

> The 'total alcoholic content' of the wine is the alcoholic content, normally expressed in per cent by volume or Gay Lussac, plus the quantity of natural sugar left in suspension in the wine expressed as potential alcohol. For very dry wines with hardly any sugar in suspension the 'total alcoholic content' would be virtually equal to the alcohol by volume. To illustrate this point further let us consider a wine with 9 degrees of alcohol by volume and 5 grams of sugar in suspension; this will have a 'total alcoholic content', known in Italian as *gradazione alcoolica complessiva*, of 11, since 5 grams of sugar, if fermented, would give 3 degrees of alcohol by volume (5 x 0·6 = 3).
>
> Furthermore, the 'natural total alcoholic content' of the wine immediately after fermentation is usually lower than the 'total alcoholic content' the wine has when sold to the consumer. This is so since correction (blending) with concentrated wine or must is often carried out to increase slightly the alcoholic content, unless otherwise stated in the regulation governing the production of each wine. It is important to remember, at this stage, that the addition of sugar (*chaptalisation*) is strictly forbidden in Italy as opposed to many other wine-producing countries in Europe and elsewhere.

The label must indicate whether a wine is a *vino da tavola*, D.O.C. or D.O.C.G., and such initials are not enough: the category must be spelled out in full. I have already explained earlier in this chapter why it is most unlikely that the initials V.Q.P.R.D., to which D.O.C. and D.O.C.G. wines are entitled (as, eventually, will *vini tipici*) will ever be used on an Italian wine label.

Most of the other regulations concerning labelling are fairly obvious; it is unnecessary here to go into detail about sizes of type and the relative placing of key words. Suffice it to say that already – or in the immediate future – the consumer is entitled to be told what grape the wine is made from, whereabouts in which country, and by whom, and whether it was bottled by individual growers or, if not, by a co-operative, in its own region or in the overseas market to which it has been shipped.

Neither the E.E.C. nor the Italian wine law forbids the paper seal of a *consorzio*, such as the black cockerel or the *putto* of the two Chianti *consorzi*, being applied over the cork, or a serial number to indicate that the bottle is one of a limited number produced in its vintage year.* I understand that when D.O.C.G. comes into effect the bottles entitled to that special *denominazione* will have a paper seal to indicate the official guarantee.

And, of course, any wine may carry a neck label indicating its vintage year – so long as it is true. But that applies to all labelling, and there is far less evasion of legal obligations than some cynics suppose.

---

* It must be borne in mind that some *consorzi* are especially singled out by the authorities as *consorzi di tutela* – authorized, that is, to apply the wine law as it refers to D.O.C. wines, to their associated members, usually the smaller growers. Other *consorzi* exist more for the protection of their members and the promotion of their products and, of course, for the maintenance of standards. A list of the *consorzi di tutela* is given in Appendix 2.

Chapter 4

Piedmont, Valle d'Aosta, Liguria

HISTORY and geography combine to give Piedmont its particularly proud and prominent place in the catalogue of Italian wines. That place, it should be explained, is not simply a matter of Piedmont's being able to boast more D.O.C. wines than any other region – this depends largely on one of the many anomalies of the D.O.C. system, which awards no fewer than seven separate *denominazioni* for Dolcetto, according to provenance, and three to Barbera, where one apiece would seem to most consumers to be enough.* The wines of Piedmont include some that have been acknowledged since long before D.O.C. as being among Italy's best. Indeed, although French wines have been so much better known than Italian wines and for so much longer, one could well say that a good Barolo, or the less well-known Ghemme and Gattinara, are among the best red wines in Europe, and to many people no sweet sparkling wine is so deliciously fresh, uncloying and fragrant as Asti Spumante. To quote Philip Dallas in his *Italian Wines* (1974), Piedmont is 'a gold-mine of fine wines'.

To understand the part played by history in giving Piedmont this special place it must be appreciated that of all the regions of Italy Piedmont is the only one not to have been occupied or ruled (save for a brief Napoleonic period) by foreign powers or an alien dynasty. This meant a more settled society in which the wine-grower could get on with his job; as Peter Nichols wrote in *Italia,*

---

* The Barbera *denominazioni* date from 1970, those of Dolcetto from 1972-4; the tendency today is generally – though not invariably – towards greater simplicity. Much depends on the parochial feeling of local growers.

Italia, 'nowhere in Italy is the making of wine taken so seriously as in Piedmont, and nowhere are such great efforts made to protect the good name of a recognised wine'. The ruling house itself set an example, even when bloody battles were being fought by Piedmontese troops (though not on Piedmontese soil) against French, Austrians and even other Italians, in the struggle for Italian unity. King Charles Albert (ruled 1831-49) took a practical interest in establishing and improving cellars and vineyards, as did his minister, and the first prime minister of united Italy, Cavour.

Piedmont's were the only regular Italian troops more or less constantly engaged in the wars of the Risorgimento (as they were, too, in the Crimea) until King Victor Emmanuel, with his dashing Piedmontese Bersaglieri, entered Rome in 1870. But the war never reached Piedmont, and just as the countryfolk were able to get on with tending their vines, so the times were quiet and prosperous enough for them to be able to sell their wine to the noblemen in their great houses and to the wealthy merchants of Turin and Genoa.

Geographically, the heartland of Piedmontese viticulture is the region's own centre: the rolling country of softly rounded hills that lies to the east of Turin (the Monferrati or Novara Hills) and the Langhe to the south. This is in the same latitude as those reaches of the Rhône that grow Hermitage and Châteauneuf du Pape, but the Piedmontese vineyards are spared the arid, stuffy wind of the Rhône, the *mistral*, that is funnelled from the south between the slopes on either side of the river. Between the great sweep of the Alps that protect it from north winds, and the much more modest but quite appreciable sub-Apennine hills just behind the Ligurian coastal strip, that form a barrier against the *mistral*, this is a sunny, smiling countryside, not sun-scorched as are the vineyards of the French Midi and the Italian Mezzogiorno, and more adapted, therefore, to produce lighter and more elegant wines (though, as will be seen in later chapters, the south of Italy, too, is learning to produce wines far less coarse and heavy than of old).

Not that the red wines of the region – and apart from Asti, Erbaluce and Cortese, this is almost entirely red-wine country – are anything but robust. Body and bouquet are the characteristics of Barolo and Barbera, Barbaresco and Dolcetto, and these wines go well with such flavoury specialities of the region as beef stewed in Barolo; *bagna cauda*, the hot garlic-and-anchovy sauce into which the Piemontesi dip crisp *crudités* and anything else that takes their fancy; and, especially, the uniquely delicious, aromatic, white, early-autumn truffles of Alba. These can be served baked in the oven – if you can afford enough of them – or used in omelettes, flaked over salads or *risotto*, or as a flavouring for the regional speciality, *fonduta* (in the local patois, *fondue*). Made with the Piedmontese cheese, *fontina*, along with the truffles, this is so tasty as to make a common or garden Swiss *fondue* seem tame indeed.

One point about Italian wines is perhaps best made in this chapter for, although it applies to Italian wines in general, it is especially applicable to those of Piedmont.

Except in Alsace, France names its wines after the regions, sub-regions, communes, villages or single vineyards in which they are grown. There is no mention of Cabernet Sauvignon or Merlot on the label of Lafite, for instance. It is styled after the property that grows it, and is also entitled to such lesser names as Pauillac, its commune and its *appellation* and, if it chose, to Médoc and to Bordeaux. Alsatian wines are named after their grape varieties: Riesling or Sylvaner or Gewürztraminer. But some Italian wines come by their names this way, some that, which is confusing. This is especially so in Piedmont, for whereas the familiar Piedmontese Barbera is a grape, Barbaresco is a commune in which a wine is made, and after which it is named, not from the Barbera but from the Nebbiolo, the classic grape that also produces the great Barolo, which should not be confused – though it often is – with the Brolio of the Chianti country, named after an estate.

One point about Italian wines is perhaps best made in this chapter

Two regions contiguous to Piedmont – Valle d'Aosta to the north and Liguria to the south – are each too small, their production of wine too modest, and their D.O.C. wines too few, to merit individual chapters. Their wines are listed here among those of Piedmont, but identified by region.

Valle d'Aosta is an Alpine region; its 110,000 inhabitants speak mostly French, or both French and Italian, or a *patois* of their own, and enjoy a considerable amount of autonomy. Here are what are said to be the highest vineyards in Europe, some of them 3,500 feet above sea-level, where grapes are picked against a glittering background of snow-capped peaks – Mont Blanc and Monte Rosa among them. Their wines are produced only in limited quantities – mountain vineyards are difficult to work, and grudging in their yield – but they have character and charm.

Liguria is little bigger in size, but has twenty times the population and produces ten times as much wine, even though the vine has to struggle for a place in the narrow coastal strip against olives and carnations, the urban overspill from Genoa and La Spezia, holiday villas and package-tour hotels.

Its wines are, on the whole, sound if not remarkable, most of them consumed in the two big cities and by Riviera holiday-makers, with the region's great range of fish dishes, and with all sorts of other foods served with *pesto*, Genoa's pungent green sauce, compounded of sweet basil, garlic, oil, nuts and cheese, alluring to the eye, fragrant to the nose, and tasty in the mouth.

D.O.C. wines of Piedmont, Valle d'Aosta and Liguria

ASTI SPUMANTE (or **ASTI** or **MOSCATO d'ASTI SPU-MANTE**) In his book, *Vino* (1980), Burton Anderson quoted me as having written in 1966 that Asti Spumante was 'generally considered too sweet for the more sophisticated English taste', and he went on to say that the recent trend in making this sparkler has been towards 'a more delicately sweet Asti Spumante than before with lightness and freshness that were not always so prominent'.

In fairness to myself I must point out that I did say 'generally considered' and added – and this Mr Anderson did not quote – that, nevertheless, Asti Spumante was 'delicious with fruit or sweets after a meal, for a mid-morning drink or at parties'. That was in 1966, and it is even truer now when, as Mr Anderson says, the trend is towards a lighter, more delicate wine.

It is made exclusively from the Moscato grape, so sweet that the necessary fermentation (which gives the bubble in the bottle) derives solely from the grape-sugar, without any further encouragement from added sugar; similarly, there is no 'liqueuring' with added sugar *after* fermentation as with most champagne in most years and with very many every year. The sweetness in the finished wine is the natural sweetness of the grape, which also gives Asti its delightful muscatel smell. One or two producers, notably Contratto, make Asti by the champagne method, but by far the most usual is the *Charmat* or *cuve close* (*autoclave*, in Italian). This involves secondary fermentation in closed vats and bottling under pressure, and is said to preserve much better the fragrance of the grape, which tends to suffer under the lengthy *méthode champenoise*: the *Charmat* system takes days rather than months.

The one *denominazione* covers a still Moscato Naturale (not usually available on the retail market, for it is more profitable to use it for the sparklers) and two sparklers: Moscato d'Asti is usually cheaper than Asti Spumante, a whisper sweeter, and 11·5° as against 12°. But these figures are misleading: 'alcohol by volume' includes natural sugar that has not been fully fermented out, and Asti has only between 7·5° and 9° 'developed'; alcoholically, it is a very light wine indeed.

BARBARESCO (12·5°) Named after the village around which it is grown, and not to be confused with Barbera, named after its grape. Referred to in Paronetto's *Guida ai Vini d'Italia* as 'the little brother' of Barolo (see below), made from the same grapes (sub-varieties of Nebbiolo) in the same way and not far away, it is similar, but a little softer and lighter in style. Said to be in line for D.O.C.G. recognition. It must be aged for two years, at least one of them in oak or chestnut-wood, before sale; after three years it may be styled *riserva*; after four, *riserva speciale*.

BARBERA d'ALBA (12°) **BARBERA d'ASTI** (12·5°)
BARBERA del MONFERRATO (11·5°) The Barbera is Pied-mont's commonest wine – twenty times as plentiful as Nebbiolo – and there are five times as much of these D.O.C. wines made from it as of Barbaresco and Barolo put together. They are good red wines, usually dry, though those of Asti and Monferrato may sometimes be slightly sweet. That of Asti is more highly regarded than the others, and there is more of it.

The first two are made exclusively from the Barbera grape, whereas the Monferrato, a lighter wine, is allowed some small admixtures; it is sometimes *frizzante*. The Alba and the Asti can be styled *superiore* if aged for three years and reaching 13°; the Monferrato at two years and 12·5°. How does one find out whether a particular bottle is quite dry or sweetish? If there is no indication on the label, ask the shopkeeper or the restaurant's *padrone*. A dry *superiore* is a treat, and not a particularly rare one: it has the depth of colour of a Barolo and its robust heartiness, without the subtlety or such capacity for ageing.

BAROLO (13°) One of the truly great wines of Italy, from the same sub-varieties of Nebbiolo as Barbaresco (see above), strong, deep in colour, flavour and smell – some say, and I wish I were as perceptive, of tar and violets, – and long-lived. Splendid with rich meat dishes, it needs opening – better still, decanting – hours before drinking. It must be aged for three years before bottling, two of them in chestnut-wood or oak; four years, and it may be styled *riserva*; five years, *riserva speciale*. The *denominazione* covers a Barolo *chinata*, made into a bitter aperitif by the addition of quinine.

BOCA (12°) Very little is made of this dry red wine – one of a number made from Nebbiolo (locally called Spanna) and other grapes in the hills between Novara and Lake Maggiore, and unlikely to be encountered elsewhere. Matured for three years before sale, two of them in wood. Others from the same district and grape are Bramaterra, Fara, Gattinara, Ghemme, Lessona and Sizzano.

BRACHETTO d'ACQUI (11·5°) Another rare red wine – light, sweetish, often slightly sparkling. Brachetto is the grape, Acqui the place it comes from – a spa town, as the name indicates, where it is prescribed to invalids and convalescents.

BRAMATERRA (12°) Same grape, same provenance, same small production as Boca (see above), from which few save local experts could distinguish it.

CALUSO See under Erbaluce (below).

CAREMA (12°) A red Nebbiolo (known locally as Pugnet, Picotener or Spanna), lighter in style than Barolo and Barbaresco, partly because of a different vinification technique, partly because it is grown between two and three thousand feet up the slopes of the valley of the Dora, almost into the Valle d'Aosta. Must be aged for four years – not in wood – before sale, but experts advise that it be drunk young once bottled.

Donnaz (see below) is the same wine from the Valle d'Aosta.

CINQUETERRE (Liguria) (11°)

CINQUETERRE SCIACCHETRA (Liguria) (13·5°) A light dry white wine that makes a good accompaniment to the shellfish landed at the five little fishing villages (*cinque terre*) of this narrow, rugged coastal strip, the picturesque charm of which has undoubtedly helped the reputation of the wine. Sciacchetra is the rare sweet version, made from the same grapes, dried. There is an even rarer, slightly stronger, *liquoroso*.

COLLI TORTONESI The red (12°) is made from the Barbera, and has the same characteristics as the Barbera wines already mentioned above. Only one-tenth as much white is produced under the *denominazione* – very light (10·5°) and dry, almost bitter, from the Cortese grape. A small proportion of this is made into a *spumante* (11·5°) of no special distinction.

CORTESE dell'ALTO MONFERRATO (10°) Similar to the white Colli Tortonesi (above) and even lighter.

DOLCEACQUA or ROSSESE di DOLCEACQUA (12°) Made from the Rossese grape, behind Ventimiglia and Bordighera, almost on the French frontier, this full-bodied, flavoury red wine belies the name of the commune it comes from ('sweet water'). It has a bitter tang beneath its dry fruitiness, and ages well. One degree more alcohol, and a year's greater age, and it may be called *superiore*.

DOLCETTO di DIANO d'ALBA (12°)   (*superiore* 12·5° and one year's ageing)

DOLCETTO d'ACQUI (11·5°)   (*superiore* 12·5° and one year's ageing)

DOLCETTO d'ALBA (11·5°)   (*superiore* 12·5° and one year's ageing)

DOLCETTO d'ASTI (11·5°)   (*superiore* 12·5° and one year's ageing)

DOLCETTO di DOGLIANI **(11·5°)**   (*superiore* 12·5° and one year's ageing)

DOLCETTO di OVADA (11·5°)   (*superiore* 12·5° and one year's ageing)

DOLCETTO delle LANGHE MONREGALESI (11°) (*superiore* 12° and one year's ageing)

There is little to choose between these firm, dry red wines, with a slightly bitter finish to their fruit (again, as with the Ligurian Dolceacqua, the name is misleading). Second, locally, only to Barbera in popularity, Dolcetto is as easy to drink as, perhaps, a young Beaujolais; sometimes, indeed, it shows the same faint youthful prickle on the tongue. The Alba and the Ovada are easily the most plentiful; the Alba is said by some to be the best, though I cannot myself find much difference between them. There is very little of the Langhe Monregalesi.

DONNAZ (VALLE d'AOSTA) The same wine as Carema (see above) from the other side of the regional frontier.

ENFER d'ARNIER (VALLE d'AOSTA) (11·5°) A dry red from Petit Rouge grapes grown in a high-walled vineyard area facing south, where the trapped heat of the sun is intense enough to give the wine its hellish name. Light aroma, intense colour, a full, forthcoming wine. Little is made, so it is rarely found outside its own district.

ERBALUCE di CALUSO (11°) **CALUSO PASSITO** (13·5°) **CALUSO PASSITO LIQUOROSO** (16°) Three separate *denominazioni* for a dry white, a naturally sweet made from semi-dried grapes, and a fortified sweet wine, all from the Erbaluce grape. The sweet and the fortified are hard to come by; the dry is delicate, with a crisp finish, and must be drunk young. Burton Anderson recommends the dry with the local trout and records with some surprise that locals like the sweet with Gorgonzola and suchlike powerful cheeses.

FARA See under Boca (above).

FREISA d'ASTI (11°) **FREISA di CHIERI** (11°) Red wines, both dry and sweet; from the Freisa grape. The dry is sharp, and shows perhaps at its best with such highly flavoured dishes as *bagna cauda*. The sweet (*amabile*) has something of a raspberry scent and is not too heavy; there is a *spumante* version of each *denominazione*, a *frizzante* of the Chieri. The dry and the *amabile* may be styled *superiore* at 11·5° with a year's ageing.

GATTINARA (12°) This is undoubtedly the best of the wines of the Novara Hills (see under Boca, above) and considered by many to be among Italy's three or four finest dry reds. Lighter in colour than the great Barolo, and less strong, but perhaps more subtle. Some detect a smell of violets; I once noted that in some bottles I found a hint of the flavour of fennel, not unpleasing but odd. Has to be aged for four years, two of them in wood, before selling.

GAVI or CORTESE di GAVI (10·5°) 'Undoubtedly the cleanest, crispest, most refreshing white wine I have come across for many a long day,' I exclaimed in an article in *Punch* in August 1981, having by some freak never met it in years of Italian travel, then stumbled upon it in a Hampshire hotel. Made from the same grape as the white Colli Tortonesi and the Cortese dell'Alto Monferrato (see above) but more elegant in style. There is a *spumante* version that still eludes me.

GHEMME (12°) Another of the Novara Hills wines (see under Boca above). Not perhaps quite so fine as Gattinara (see above), having only 60-85 per cent Nebbiolo as against Gattinara's minimum of 80 per cent, but a cut above the others; ages well.

GRIGNOLINO d'ASTI (11°)
GRIGNOLINO del MONFERRATO CASALESE (11°) Light dry reds, from the grape of the same name, with a pleasantly fresh bouquet, more like the light wines of the Veneto, such as Bardolino, than the more robust reds of its own region, and usually drunk young and cool.

LESSONA See under Boca (above).

MALVASIA di CASORZO d'ASTI (10·5°)
MALVASIA di CASTELNUOVO DON BOSCO (10·5°) Light sweet and sweetish red wines, very like Brachetto (above); sometimes sparkling.

NEBBIOLO d'ALBA (12°) The same grape that goes into the great wines of the region: Barolo, Barbaresco, Gattinara and such like. This Nebbiolo from a delimited area around Cuneo, if not quite in their class, is worthy of its name. A sturdy red wine, it is not unlike Barolo, and sometimes, pleasingly, a little fruitier at the finish. A little *dolce* and *spumante* are made.

RUBINO di CANTAVENNA (11·5°) In effect, a Barbera (see above), and so little is produced that it is difficult to understand how it comes to have a *denominazione* of its own.

SIZZANO (11·5°) Another of the Novara Hills wines (see under Boca, above). Comes from very near Ghemme and Gattinara, but not so distinguished as either, having less Nebbiolo in its blend.

Other wines of Piedmont, Valle d'Aosta and Liguria

ARCOLA (LIGURIA) Simple red and white table wines produced between La Spezia and Lerici and consumed locally.

ARNEIS Light, dry, white wine from near Alba, becoming well-known and highly regarded, made from grape of the same name.

BARBAROSSA (LIGURIA) Pink wine (unusual in these parts) and some red, from local vine of the same name, so-called because the long bunches of grapes that it bears look like long red beards. Grown, and drunk, on the holiday coast on either side of Finale Ligure.

BARBERA della VAL TIGLIONE

BARBERA delle COLLINE PIEDMONTESE Good examples, though not D.O.C., of the region's best-known red wine (see Barbera, above).

BARENGO Straw-coloured, dry white wine, rather strong, from near Novara. I think there is also a sweet version, and a red, from the Bonarda grape.

BLANC de MORGEX (VALLE d'AOSTA) Dry white wine made from local varieties of grape in mountain vineyards, some 3,000 feet above sea-level. Scent and taste of herbs.

BUZZETTO (LIGURIA) Local dry white wine, drunk *all'annata*.

CAMPOCHIESA (LIGURIA) Full, fragrant but dry white, a rarity among dry white wines in its capacity for ageing; indeed, locals are said to put down a demijohn when a son is born, to drink at his wedding.

CORONATA (LIGURIA) Like Buzzetto (above). Hint of lemon flavour.

CORTESE (LIGURIA) Similar to D.O.C. Cortese wines of Piedmont (see above), but rather stronger and coarser.

DOLCETTO (PIEDMONT and LIGURIA) Various local wines similar in style if not always in quality to those of Piedmont with D.O.C. status (see Dolcetto, above).

FAVORITA Light, dry white from native grape near Alba. Bitter-almond back-taste.

FREISA Humbler relatives of the D.O.C. Freisas (see above).

GAMAY (VALLE d'AOSTA) Sturdy red from the Beaujolais grape.

LUMASSINA (LIGURIA) Very similar to Buzzetto (see above).

MARINASCO (LIGURIA) Dry and semi-sweet whites from the Trebbiano grape.

NEBBIOLO The grape that gives us Barolo always produces sound, decent red wine, even when non-D.O.C.

PETIT ROUGE (VALLE d'AOSTA) Fairly full, well-rounded red.

PIGATO (LIGURIA) Sound dry white wine – one of the most reliable in the fish restaurants of the Italian Riviera.

PINOT GRIS (VALLE d'AOSTA) Dry white, rather neutral.

POLCEVERA (LIGURIA) Similar to Buzzetto (see above).

ROSATO di PIETRA LIGURE (LIGURIA) One of the Barbarossa pinks (see above).

ROSSESE di ALBENGA (LIGURIA) Another Ligurian pink, from the same grape as in Dolceacqua (see above); deeper in colour and flavour than the Rosato above.

VERMENTINO (LIGURIA) Similar to Pigato (above), though from a different grape and perhaps not quite so good.

Chapter 5

Lombardy

WITH the same area as Piedmont, almost to the square inch, and very nearly twice the population, Lombardy produces less than half as much wine (and only one third as many of D.O.C. status), for a high proportion of its nearly nine million inhabitants work in the factories of Milan or the ricefields of the Po Valley.

There are good wines made here, though – some of them well-known but underrated because, as Burton Anderson has observed, 'some perfectly lovely wines made in the area around Lakes Maggiore, Varese and Como never make it into bottle. They are served by the carafe in restaurants and bars, or toted off in demijohns by city dwellers who like to boast of a *vino quotidiano* that draws from friends compliments to their good taste.'

If the number of D.O.C. wines seems small even in relation to the modest overall production, this is largely, if not entirely, owing to one of the anomalies of the D.O.C. system: among the wines of Lombardy there are several, of different colours, with different characteristics, and made from different grapes, that are all entitled to the one *denominazione*, Oltrepò Pavese. In Piedmont, by contrast, there are three wines, all red, and all made from the same grape, the Barbera, but each with a *denominazione* of its own, and no fewer than seven Dolcetto wines, similarly related to each other, but each with its distinct *denominazione*.

Because most of the fine wines of Lombardy – and the best of them are especially fine – are each made in small quantities, barely enough to supply the tables of Milanese tycoons and the elegant restaurants of the lake resorts, not to mention the well-heeled connoisseurs of next-door Switzerland (always on the look-out for good reds, especially) few of them reach the United Kingdom or the United States. In their native region, though, they are well worth looking for: the red wines, for instance, that bear the

51

denominazione Valtellina or, especially, Valtellina Superiore, with Milanese cutlets or *osso bucco* or the various rich *risotti* of the region; such whites as Lugano or one of the Rieslings of the Oltrepò with the carp, pike or perch of Como or Garda.

D.O.C. wines of Lombardy

BOTTICINO (12°) A clear, bright red wine, with more than a hint of sweetness, from the little town of Botticino, between the southernmost tip of Lake Garda and the industrialized but still handsome city of Brescia, where most of it is drunk, young and cool. Largely from Barbera grapes, with a certain amount of Sangiovese, the aristocratic grape of Chianti, and a little of others.

CAPRIANO del COLLE (11°) A red and a white, from south of Brescia. The red is made from a blend chiefly of Sangiovese and Marzemino, the white from Trebbiano; it is usually called Capriano del Colle-Trebbiano in full, though one *denominazione* covers both wines. There is little of either about, and plenty of other, more interesting, wines.

CELLATICO (11·5°) Also named after a small town near Brescia in the same district as Botticino (above). Similar in style, though less strong and rather drier, made with more of the Schiava grape.

COLLI MORENICI MANTOVANI del GARDA (11°) These are the hills that run from the southern end of Lake Garda to the city of Mantua, their vineyards linking up with those of neighbouring Veneto, such as the Bardolino, which the reds here resemble, though they can range from a *rosato* to a rather deeper, but still pink *chiaretto* to a *rubino*.

The white is not unlike Soave (see chapter 7), being made from the same grape; it is credited by Felice Cùnsolo with a fragrance as of lemons, which I would welcome could I find it myself.

I remember when some of the wines here were known generically as *vini del Serraglio*, which I thought exotically evocative until I learned that the Serraglio here is merely a place-name: historians and others will recognize the name of one of the wine-growing communes – Solferino – where the sufferings of the wounded after the battle of 1859 so moved Jean-Henri Dunant as to lead to the foundation of the Red Cross.

FRANCIACORTA One *denominazione* for a red and a white. The red (11°), from a blend chiefly of Cabernet Franc and Barbera, with some Nebbiolo and Merlot, is a stylish light wine, to drink young and cool. The dry white (11·5°), from Pinot Bianco, is particularly good. The *denominazione* also covers a *spumante* version, champagne-method, that is one of Italy's best.

LUGANA (11·5°) From the Trebbiano grape, once called locally Torbiano, but now Trebbiano di Lugano because of the distinction earned by this wine from near the town of that name at the southern end of Lake Garda, near Tennyson's Desenzano. Light gold in colour, perhaps because of some ageing in wood, though this does not coarsen it; it is delicious with the local lake fish. The D.O.C. zone reaches into the Veneto (indeed, 'Veronese' is sometimes tacked on to the grape name), but the wine is credited to Lombardy in the official list.

OLTREPÒ PAVESE A real portmanteau of a *denominazione*, accommodating no fewer than ten distinct wines, what they have in common being that all are from the Oltrepò Pavese, that part of the province of Pavia that lies to the south, in the hilly country on the other side of the Po from the city of Pavia itself. This is a region of big, efficient co-operatives and dedicated small-scale growers who, between them, have been setting standards of quality and consistency for half a century.

It is best here to list the ten wines separately:

Oltrepò Pavese-Barbacarlo (12°) Named after a local commune, made chiefly from Barbera and Croatina; a deep red, slightly sweet, often fizzy, very fruity.

Oltrepò Pavese-Barbera (11·5°) Like the Barbera of Piedmont (see chapter 4), though perhaps rather lighter in body. By a long chalk the most plentiful of the Oltrepò wines, red or white.

Oltrepò Pavese-Bonarda (11°) From the same grape as the Bonarda wine of Emilia-Romagna (see chapter 9), which it resembles.

Oltrepò Pavese-Buttafuoco (12°) Chiefly from Barbera and Croatina grapes; a dry red wine. Like the Barbacarlo, though it is usually drier, it froths when first poured out – hence its name, for it is said to crackle like *fuoco*, fire – and then settles down into a typical, easy to drink, Oltrepò red.

Oltrepò Pavese-Cortese (11°) White, from the Cortese grape, crisply sharp in the mouth, with a family resemblance to, but not quite the distinction of, the Gavi wines of Piedmont (see chapter 4).

53

Oltrepò Pavese-Moscato (10·5°) Because the general standard of wine-making in the Oltrepò Pavese is so high the sweet white Moscato of the district, with its rich bouquet, ranks high among the many from the same grape made pretty well all over Italy. The sparkling version is little inferior, if at all, to that of Piedmont.

Oltrepò Pavese-Pinot (11°) The *denominazione* covers red, white and *rosato* – there is a white and a *rosato spumante*, very good. From Pinot Grigio or Pinot Nero, according to colour.

Oltrepò Pavese-Riesling (11°) A blend of the Renano and the Italico Rieslings, fresh and fragrant; makes a good *spumante*.

Oltrepò Pavese-Rosso (11·5°) The only Oltrepò Pavese wine that is not a varietal (a wine exclusively from one named grape): it may be made of a blend of the usual red-wine grapes of the district. Good, because this is a district of well-made wines, but I would prefer a Bonardo or Barbera, myself.

Oltrepò Pavese-Sangue di Giuda (12°) A sweet red that froths when poured out, like its drier red Oltrepò relatives. Very little is made, and I do not mind.

RIVIERA del GARDA BRESCIANO Red and *rosato* (or *chiaretto*) wines made on the western shore of Lake Garda. The Groppello grape is predominant in a blend that also includes Barbera, Sangiovese and Marzemino (here often called Barzemino). There is little difference between the red and the pink wines save that, oddly enough, the pink is stronger than the red – 11·5° as against 11°. But with an extra year's ageing and a minimum of 12°, the red can be styled *superiore*, and this does not apply to the pink.

The pink is deep in colour, the red light. Both are cheerful wines, easy to drink, like the nearby lakeside wines of the Veneto.

TOCAI di SAN MARTINO della BATTAGLIA (12°) A white wine from near Lugana; as with Lugana, the D.O.C. zone reaches into the Veneto, but official lists credit it solely to Lombardy. The Tocai grape was introduced from Friuli-Venezia Giulia only as recently as the beginning of the century and the wine is only now becoming known outside its own area. It is a flavoury, refreshing dry wine, perhaps – it seems to me – a shade sweeter than the Tocai of Friuli, or it may be that there is a less noticeable bitterness in the after-taste.

VALCALEPIO A white (11·5°) and a red (12°), relative newcomers to the D.O.C. ranks, from near Bergamo, the lively town where both the *commedia dell' arte* and the composer Donizetti were born. The white, very little of which is produced, is from Pinot Bianco and Pinot Grigio, dry and full, usually drunk very young.

The red, from Merlot and Cabernet Sauvignon, the former predominating, is, as might be expected, not unlike a claret in style, but rather bigger than most; official publications recommend opening it some time before serving.

VALTELLINA (11°) VALTELLINA SUPERIORE (12°)

Valtellina is the name given to the sub-Alpine valley formed by the Adda river, flowing from east to west into Lake Como, only just inside the frontier with Switzerland. Indeed, some of the owners and tenders of these Italian vineyards are Swiss; they are allowed to take their wines across the frontier duty-free, and the fine reds of the district (see below, under Valtellina Superiore) are great favourites of the Swiss, who lack red wines of their own of similar quality.

The one *denominazione* covers both wines and, under Valtellina Superiore, four wines usually known by their own, individual names.

The steep northern bank of the Adda, stretching on either side of the town of Sondrio, is terraced with vineyards up to a couple of thousand feet above sea-level, the vines benefiting from the southern aspect, the sunshine intensified by reflection from the surface of the river.

The important grape is the Nebbiolo (also known here as the Chiavennasca), from which also derive such great Piedmontese wines as Barolo and Gattinara (see chapter 4). If the Valtellina wines do not attain quite the same quality as these, or the Valtellina Superiore, it may be partly because of soil and altitude but also, and more especially, because they are permitted up to 30 per cent of other grapes compared with Barolo's none, Gattinara's 10, and the Valtellina Superiore wines' 5.

Of the Valtellina wines, the odd one out is Sfursat (a dialect corruption of Sforzato), made of part-dried grapes and becoming, like the Valpolicella Recioto-Amarone of the Veneto (see chapter 7), a richer, fuller, rounder wine – stronger, too: 14·5°.

The Valtellina Superiore wines are: **Inferno, Grumello, Sassella and Valgella** – all typical Nebbiolo wines. If not so famous as their Piedmontese relatives, the family resemblance is clear. I have sometimes thought that their best bottles, at any rate, have a clearer colour and a prettier bouquet.

All need ageing – at least two to three years in cask, according to Burton Anderson, who holds that in good years they deserve six to twelve more in bottle. The Sassella (the name is misleading, being that of a grape whereas, like the others, this is a Nebbiolo wine with at most 5 per cent of Sassella) is said to be coarser than the others when young but all the better when mature; the Grumello is said by some to be softer, and the Inferno nuttier in flavour. But such differences are, as I have said, minimal; they may, indeed, be imaginary or, at any rate, subjective. They are all wines of great character and, being less well-known, often better value for money than the great reds of Piedmont.

Other wines of Lombardy

ANGERA Red wine, fruity in flavour, from a blend of Barbera, Bonarda and Nebbiolo grapes; comes from the extreme north-west of the region, outside the main wine-growing areas, near Lake Varese, between Como and Maggiore, where most of it is consumed.

BIANCO di MAGUZZANO White wine, also from the lake district, and mostly drunk there. Dry but full; local enthusiasts claim to find the scents of bread crust, gorse flowers, and fresh almonds.

BOSNASCO Dryish to sweetish, slightly *frizzante* white wine from the Cortese grape. Always drunk young, and usually as an aperitif.

CANNETO An *amaro* and *dolce* red made from the usual blend of Oltrepò grapes, but vinified to be *frizzante*, a little like the Lambrusco of Emilia-Romagna (see chapter 9).

CASTEGGIO BIANCO A wide range of dry, refreshing white wines from the Oltrepò.

CHIARETTO del LAGO d'ISEO Dry, deep pink wine to be drunk young; very like a lighter version of Groppello (see below) from the nearby Riviera del Garda.

GROPPELLO della VALTENESI Dry red wine from the Valtenesi, just inland from the westward shore of Lake Garda. Made in much the same way as Chianti, but not so full in flavour.

PUSTERLA Red, white and *rosato* wines from near Brescia; all fairly bland, country wines, mostly consumed young and in the district.

ROSSO di BELLAGIO Well-made, well-bred red wine from near the handsome Lake Como resort, from a blend of noble French grapes: Cabernet Sauvignon, Cabernet Franc, Merlot, Malbec and Pinot Noir.

SAN COLOMBANO Sometimes sweetish, sometimes dryish, usually *frizzante* red from almost the very outskirts of Milan. Burton Anderson likes it more than I do.

Chapter 6

Trentino-Alto Adige

THIS composite region – the southern part, the province of
Trento, Italian, and the northern part, the Alto Adige, which is the
province of Bolzano, German-speaking – was under Austrian rule
until 1919. Now this northernmost region of Italy has a
considerable measure of autonomy because of the big Germanic
minority, deeply conscious of its language and its culture. (What the
Italian government did not permit, for strategic reasons, was a
separate status for the German-speaking Alto Adige similar to that
enjoyed by the French-speaking Valle d'Aosta: a joint autonomous
Trentino-Alto Adige gave a considerable measure of self-
government, but to a region with an Italian majority.)

Although something like three-quarters of the wine produced in
the Alto Adige is red, which seems very un-German – or un-
Austrian – one has a feeling that cultural differences are reflected in
the wines. Those from the Alto Adige usually bear German names
(both languages or either are permitted on labels), as do their
growers; you taste them in trim *Weinstuben* with German- or
Austrian-looking gables and timbering; Germany and Austria and
Switzerland import them, and drink them as though they were the
red wines that they would grow themselves if their climates
permitted. (The Alto Adige is Alpine country, and vines are grown
here up to the snow-line, but it enjoys more of the ripening sunshine
that red wines need than the Alpine regions to the north.) And one
drinks them here with boiled beef and cooked sausages, dumplings
and cabbage dishes, and – the sweet ones – with strudels.

Although, when they compare themselves with the Alto Atesini, the people of the southern province, Trento, undoubtedly regard themselves as Italian – indeed, *Italianissimi* – they have a rather detached attitude towards the rest of Italy, almost, if not quite so much, as the islanders of Sicily and Sardinia do, or the Venetians, who are Veneziani first, Italians some way after. It may be because many now alive – most of their fathers, in any case – were born under Austrian rule; Trento became Italian more recently than any other part of Italy. The influence on their wine-growing, though, is at least as much French as Austrian: Cabernets and Merlots and Pinots are grown here as prolifically and as successfully as the Rieslings both of Germany and Italy, and the Veltliner of Austria. (French vines make something of a showing in the Alto Adige, too, but more modestly.) What is surprising is that there has been no attempt to grow the varieties that make such good wines in the next-door regions of Italy, such as the Barbera and Cortese of Lombardy, and the Sangiovese and Trebbiano of Emilia-Romagna.

The way in which *denominazioni* have been awarded here is like that in the other composite region to the east, Friuli-Venezia Giulia, with varieties of grape being grouped under a geographical heading, and pretty confusing it is – more so in the Alto Adige than in Trento. Indeed, Burton Anderson maintains that it not only confuses consumers but serves to discourage some growers from applying for D.O.C. status. In the following lists I have given the wines of the two wine-growing provinces of the region separately to minimize confusion.

The region as a whole, though not so productive as others, is top of the table for D.O.C. wines (more than 55 per cent of the total) and, thanks especially to wines from the Alto Adige that are sold to Germany, Austria and Switzerland, in wines, D.O.C. and non-D.O.C., shipped abroad (about 35 per cent).

D.O.C. *wines of the Alto Adige*

ALTO ADIGE or SUDTIROL There are sixteen different varietal names under this portmanteau *denominazione*, and some of them cover more than one wine – for instance, Lagrein can be Lagrein Rosato, pink, or Lagrein Scuro, red. For that matter, it can be labelled Lagrein Kretzer or Lagrein Dunkel and, if produced in the province of Bolzano, Lagrein di Gries or Grieser Lagrein. The following list is as simple as I can make it: I hope that my attempt at simplicity will not lead to further mystification.

For D.O.C. status, each of these varietal wines must be from 95 per cent of the grapes named, except for Schiava, 85 per cent.

According to Philip Dallas in the Italian chapter of *Wines of the World*, the Alto Adige D.O.C. whites are grown at more than 2,700 feet above sea-level, the reds at 2,100 feet.

Alto Adige or Sudtirol Cabernet (11·5°) From Cabernet Sauvignon or Cabernet Franc or both; one of the best red wines of the region, with quite a touch of claret about it.

Alto Adigo or Sudtirol Lagrein (11·5°) See above for variations on the name. Much less red (Scuro or Dunkel) is produced than the pink (Rosato or Kretzer) which is deep in colour, fresh and sometimes a little prickly on the tongue; understandably the most popular wine in the region.

Alto Adige or Sudtirol Malvasia or Malvasier (11·5°) Very little is made of this rich red dessert (or, locally, aperitif) wine.

Alto Adige or Sudtirol Merlot (11°) More than twice as much Merlot as Cabernet is grown in the Alto Adige. It makes a rather softer wine, also with more than a hint of claret about it, but does not age so well.

Alto Adige or Sudtirol Moscato Giallo or Goldenmuskateller (10·5°) Sweet golden dessert wine, but not richly heavy.

Alto Adige or Sudtirol Moscato Rosa or Rosenmuskateller (12°) Fuller than the above, more fragrant and stronger, partly because the must is kept longer on the skins, partly because yield per hectare is more severely limited by law (60 as against 80 quintals).

Alto Adige or Sudtirol Pinot Bianco or Weissburgunder (11°) Second only to the Lagrein Rosato as the most plentiful and popular wine of the Alto Adige. Sound, consistent and eminently drinkable; although its *denominazione* gives it higher rank, I would class it as a very good *vin ordinaire* – but mean it as a compliment.

Alto Adige or Sudtirol Pinot Grigio or Rülander (11·5°) Dry white wine, not outstanding, to be drunk young, when it is often *frizzante*.

Alto Adige or Sudtirol Pinot Nero or Blauburgunder (11°) Full, big red wine, clearly recognizable as coming from the great Burgundy grape. One year's extra ageing, and it may be styled *riserva*.

Alto Adige or Sudtirol Riesling Italico or Welschriesling (11°) Much less of this is grown and drunk than of the Riesling Renano (see below) – and understandably. As David Peppercorn observes in his *Drinking Wine*, it lacks 'the distinctive fruit-acidity of the authentic Rhine riesling'.

Alto Adige or Sudtirol Riesling Renano or Rheinriesling (11°) More of it than the Italico (above) and better, if not quite so prettily appealing to the nose as Alsace and Moselle wines from the same grape. But the style is there.

Alto Adige or Sudtirol Riesling Silvaner or Müller-Thurgau (11°) A newcomer to this *denominazione* – an aromatic white, well-known to amateurs of German and English wines. Not much grown but worth looking for in the restaurants of Bolzano.

Alto Adige or Sudtirol Sauvignon (11·5°) Very little indeed made of this wine from the versatile grape that makes both the crisp whites of the Loire and (with the Sémillon) the sweet whites of Bordeaux. Here, a full-flavoured, almost spicy, white wine.

Alto Adige or Sudtirol Schiava or Vernatsch (10·5°) The lightest, in texture and in colour, of the region's reds, with a pronounced scent and a sort of nuttiness to the taste.

Alto Adige or Sudtirol Silvaner (11°) Little is produced of this light, rather bland white wine, similar to the Sylvaner of Alsace (note the difference in spelling); not so interesting as the Riesling Renano.

Alto Adige or Sudtirol Traminer Aromatico or Gewürztraminer (11·5°) The Traminer of Germany and Alsace is said to have originated in, and derived its name from, the village of Tramin (Termeno, in Italian) between Bolzano and Trento, in the south of the Alto Adige. Here, on its home ground, it is not perhaps so aromatic as in its adopted countries, but it is a satisfying drink, and obviously a wine of breeding.

CALDARO or LAGO di CALDARO or KALTERER or KALTERERSEE (10·5°) Enormous amounts are grown of this light refreshing red wine around Lake Caldaro – much better known to the locals and to the Austrian, German, and German-speaking Swiss visitors and wine-shippers as Kalterersee. Made from sub-varieties of the Schiava grape. Above 11°, it may be styled *scelto* (selected) or *Auslese*, and, if from a central demarcated area, *classico*.

COLLI di BOLZANO or BOZNER LEITEN (11°) Virtually the same as the above, and very like the Alto Adige Schiava (see above) but perhaps somewhat fuller.

MERANESE or MERANESE di COLLINA or MERANER HÜGEL (10·5°) Yet another of the Schiava family of lightish reds. There is a sort of *classico* from the middle of the zone that may be labelled *Burgravio* or *Burggrafier*.

SANTA MADDALENA or ST MAGDALENER (11·5°) Ten years later, Bruno Roncarati quoted my judgment of 1966 that this is 'the finest of the red wines of the region . . . deeper in colour and fuller in flavour than the Caldaro wines'; now, five years later still, this remains my opinion. Mostly made of Schiava, like the Caldaro wines, it derives greater intensity from it because (like the great hocks of the Rheingau) it benefits not only from being grown on the northern, that is to say, south-facing bank of an east-west flowing river, in this case the Isarco, but also from the warm sunshine reflected by the water. Up to 10 per cent of other grapes is permitted, for additional body. There is a *classico* (*Klassisches Ursprungsgebiet*) zone.

TERLANO or TERLANER The *denominazione* applies to seven white wines grown in the pretty countryside that has as its central wine-making town Terlano, west of Bolzano; this is in effect the white-wine section of the zone of which Caldaro is the red-wine section. The wines are:

Terlano (11·5°) A blend of the white grapes of the zone, of which Pinot Bianco must provide 50 per cent.

Terlano-Pinot Bianco (11°) For this, 90 per cent of the named grape is required. (See under Alto Adige Pinot Bianco above.)

Terlano-Riesling Italico (10·5°) As with all the others, save the Terlano itself, 90 per cent of the named grape is required.

Terlano-Riesling Renano (11·5°) Much less is made than of the Italico, though to my mind this is much the more interesting wine.

Terlano-Sauvignon (12°) Strongest of the range, and perhaps the most flavoury.

Terlano-Silvaner (11·5°) Resembles that of the Alto Adige *denominazioni*, but less bland.

Terlano-Müller-Thurgau (11°) See under Alto Adige: it resembles the wine of that zone both in style and in scarcity.

There is not much to be said of these wines individually, as there is a close family resemblance, in spite of the difference in the grapes and their relative truth to type. David Peppercorn considers them all full-bodied, the Italico perhaps the least so. My own preference *in this particular range* is for the Pinot Bianco – rather to my own surprise, for in other wine-growing countries the Rhine Riesling would be more to my taste. But I may have been luckier in individual bottles of the one than of the other. There is a demarcated central *classico* zone common to all the wines, so that each may be a *classico* or not.

VALLE ISARCO or EISACKTALER The *denominazione* covers five white varietals from the valley of the Isarco river, all German in style (except the Pinot Grigio, of which little is made, anyway) as befits this especially Germanic part of the German-speaking Alto Adige. Little need be said of them individually – they run true to type as exemplified by the wines already listed under group *denominazioni*:

Valle Isarco or Eisacktaler Traminer Aromatico (11°) Very little made.

Valle Isarco or Eisacktaler Pinot Grigio (11°) Very little made.

Valle Isarco or Eisacktaler Veltliner (10°) This is the only example I know of this interesting Austrian vine's being grown in Italy, at any rate to D.O.C. standard. Again, very little is made – a pity, for it is fresh and spicy to the taste.

Valle Isarco or Eisacktaler Silvaner (10·5°) Here is the explanation of all those repetitions of 'very little made': this agreeably soft, highly drinkable wine accounts for more than three-quarters of the Valle Isarco D.O.C. production, and understandably so.

Valle Isarco or Eisacktaler Müller-Thurgau (10·5°) Typically aromatic but rather light in body compared with wines made elsewhere from this grape.

Note that as in the Alto Adige D.O.C. wines, these varieties may be labelled in German – note, too, that this would change Sylvaner to Silvaner, which may explain why there seem to be inconsistencies in the text of this book.

D.O.C. wines of Trentino

THERE are fewer types of wine in this Italian-speaking southern part of the composite region: variety for variety, it is probably true that, as Philip Dallas has pointed out in his *Italian Wines*, they tend to have more body and less bouquet than those of the Alto Adige. I would not disagree, but consider that the differences are pretty marginal, in most cases noticeable only when comparable wines are tasted side by side – and we seldom have the chance to make such comparisons.

CASTELLER (11°) A great deal is produced of this day-to-day wine of the citizens of Trento and its surroundings – a blend of Schiava, Merlot and Lambrusco that ranges from deepest *rosato* to lightest red. Although it seems a commonplace in its own zone, it deserves its *denominazione* for its consistency and easy charm.

SORNI There is a red (10·5°) and a white (10°). The white is made chiefly from the Nosiola grape, which seems to be peculiar to the district; it is soft but refreshing, especially when drunk very young. So too the red – there is five times as much – which is light, dry and with a pronounced nose, made chiefly from the Schiava grape. A favourite in Switzerland.

TEROLDOGO ROTALIANO (11·5°) As with Casteller (above) there is a lot of this about, in and around the city of Trento; unlike the Casteller, it is a big, hearty, robust red wine – Casteller's big brother, so to speak – full of flavour, with a rather bitter after-taste. From the grape of the same name.

TRENTINO Like the Alto Adige *denominazione*, this covers a range of varietals – ten, compared with the sixteen of the northern province:

Cabernet Trentino (11·5°) Much more Cabernet is made here than in the Alto Adige. It resembles that of the Alto Adige (see above), though experts may detect, as Philip Dallas did, more body, less bouquet.

Lagrein Trentino (11°) More is produced of this lighter red wine – lighter in colour and in substance – than of the Cabernet. As in the Alto Adige, it ranges from *rosato* to red. Two years' ageing and 11·5° for a *riserva*.

Marzemino Trentino (11°) This red wine is a long-standing favourite in the district round Trento, where it is a local grape. Lightish rather than full, with a bitter-almond finish, it is quite dry, though some social historians believe that it was on the sweetish side when Lorenzo da Ponte, the librettist, wrote in Mozart's *Don Giovanni* of '*l'eccelente Marzemino.*'

Merlot Trentino (11°) The most plentiful of the Trentino wines, as is the Merlot of those of the Alto Adige, which it closely

Moscato grapes grown in Piedmont for Asti Spumante

Vines high in the hills at Carema in Piedmont. The colonnades are distinctive of this region

Cinqueterre vines growing on the steep coastal slopes of Liguria

Santa Maddalena vineyards in the Alto Adige, growing 'the finest of the red wines of the region . . .'

*Malvasia vines at
Casatico in Emilia
Romagna. In the
background is the
fifteenth-century
castle of Torrechiara
(Photo G. Mondelli)
Below: harvesting the
Malvasia grapes on the
Parmensi Hills at
Pieve di Cusignano
(Photo G. Mondelli)*

Harvesting in Apulia—a region which produces more wine than any other

Vineyards in Lombardy

Wine-growing slopes in the area of Fano in Marche. Above: some grapes from the region

Vineyards in the Veneto for the production of Soave, the highest-selling D.O.C. white wine in the United Kingdom.

A Chianti Classico vineyard in the heartland of Tuscany

Grapes used in the production of Corvo wines from the estate in Sicily

A vineyard in Lazio, producing Marino

Orvieto vines in Umbria

resembles; a soft, dry, red wine, easy to drink. Not so suitable for ageing as the Cabernet, but with two years' ageing and 11·5° it is entitled to call itself *riserva*.

Moscato Trentino (13°) Sweet, golden dessert wine; fuller than that of the Alto Adige, and more of it.

Pinot Trentino (11°) Half Pinot Bianco, half Pinot Grigio, this dry white wine goes mostly to the making of *spumante*, also entitled to the *denominazione*. Some examples from this region are outstanding. (See Appendix 1.)

Pinot Nero Trentino (11·5°) There is not much of this biggish dry red wine, which is fuller and stronger than its blood-brother from the Alto Adige, and more suitable for ageing: it must have two years' ageing and reach 12° to become a *riserva*, as against one year and the original 11° for the Alto Adige.

Riesling Trentino (11°) May be made of Riesling Renano, Riesling Italico or Riesling-Silvaner, separately or together, unlike those of the Alto Adige, one of which is Renano, one Italico. This is usually biggish and flavoury, but not so refreshingly fruit-acid balanced as most rieslings.

Vin Santo Trentino (14°) Those who like this kind of rich dessert wine (see Appendix 1) consider the *vin santo* of Trentino to be probably Italy's best. Aged in cask for at least three years, it has some delicacy to its lusciousness.

VALDADIGE or ELTSCHTALER The white (10·5°) and the red (11°) of both provinces of the region, Trento and Bolzano – in other words, of both the Italian-speaking and German-speaking zones, hence the alternative names. The whites are from blends of ten varieties of grape or from any one or more of them. The red must be at least 20 per cent Schiava and 10 per cent Lambrusco, the balance being made up from half a dozen others. Great quantities are produced; much is drunk by the glass or the carafe locally, much (especially of the red) exported. The red is light and nutty, the white light and unassuming.

Other wines of Trentino-Alto Adige

MARZEMINO di ISERA Without a *denominazione* but, to me, indistinguishable from the D.O.C. Marzemino Trentino (see above). Retains a separate identity as being made from a distinct local sub-variety of the grape. From the Vallagrina area (see below).

MÜLLER-THURGAU della VALLE dei LAGHE Similar to that of the Alto Adige *denominazione* (see above).

SCHIAVA ATESINA See under Alto Adige. This is the same wine produced in various parts of the region not – or not yet – registered as eligible for D.O.C.

TOBLINO The red, Castel Toblino, resembles the Schiava, above; the white, Nosiola di Toblino, resembles the white Sorni (above).

VALLAGRINA From the Adige valley in the middle of the region, near Trento, three wines without *denominazione*, but of quality:
    Cabernet della Vallagrina Made mostly of Cabernet Franc with a little Cabernet Sauvignon; in the same class as the Trentino Cabernet.
    Merlot della Vallagrina Also to be compared with the Trentino D.O.C. wine.
    Lambrusco della Vallagrina Made around Rovereto, south of Trento, a dry, frothy red wine like the dry Lambruschi of Emilia-Romagna (see chapter 9). Best drunk within six months of the vintage: I would drink it cool, but the locals do not.

Chapter 7

The Veneto

SCENICALLY, sociologically and economically, the Veneto is a vastly varied region. It stretches from the pretty and, in some parts, over-prettified shores of Lake Garda to the Venetian lagoon, from the ice-capped peaks of the Dolomites to the paddy-fields of the Po. Not every Veneziano is rich, as any of the peasants of the Po delta will tell you, but there are riches in the region. Once, they were from the gorgeous East that the republic of Venice held in fee – the riches that built the palaces that line the Grand Canal and the Palladian villas along the Brenta; now it is tourist money, not only from the art-lovers and pleasure-seekers and idlers from abroad who flock to the Lakes, to Venice, to Vicenza, Verona and Padua, and the ski-slopes of Cortina, but from visiting Milanesi and Torinesi, too.

So there has always been a demand here for wine – long before the Venetian heyday, indeed, when Virgil on his Mantuan farm and Catullus at his Sirmione villa drank the Rhaetic that grew where Soave grows today. The slopes of Lake Garda's eastern shore, of the Piave valley and of the hills between Vicenza and Verona – almost everywhere in the region save the plains of the Po – make good vineyard country, and many of the locals and most of the visitors have the taste and judgement to ask for drinkable and consistent wines, and the money to pay for them.

So, too, the foreigners who flock to these seductive parts ask, when they get back home, for the wines they enjoyed at lakeside picnics or in Venice restaurants: the red wines of Garda, particularly, are much in demand in Germany, Austria and Switzerland; Valpolicella, in the United States and Britain.

Not that any of the Veneto's red wines – not even the best Valpolicella Amarone – in my opinion, at any rate, reaches the same degree of distinction as such great wines of other regions as the

Barolo of Piedmont or the Brunello of Tuscany, but they are well-made, consistent, immediately pleasing in style and Soave at its best is one of the great white wines of Italy and – happily – there is plenty of it, so that it is not, or should not be, expensive. So, too, with the reds: there is ten times as much Valpolicella as there is Barolo, ten times as much Bardolino as Brunello.

D.O.C. wines of the Veneto

BARDOLINO (10·5°) No discordant note in the Italian wine-writers' acclaim for Bardolino: 'jolly' says Monelli; *'simpatico'* and 'joyous' according to Veronelli.

I would not perhaps go so far as Zeffiro Bocci's 'wine of friendship and young, sweet and carefree love', but I feel great affection for this light, fruity, red wine, and not only because I drank it, long ago, with Max Beerbohm at his villa at Rapallo.

The grapes are Corvina (for body and colour), Rondinella (flavour), Rossara (fragrance) and Negrara (softness) – the same that go to make Valpolicella (see below) and in virtually the same proportions. That Bardolino is lighter, Valpolicella fuller, is due, partly at any rate, to Bardolino's sandy, gravelly soil and Valpolicella's clay.

Bardolino may add *classico* to its *denominazione* if it comes from the original central zone of production; Bardolino Chiaretto is more of a pink than a red, the must having been taken quickly off the skins; and the wine becomes *superiore* if it reaches 11·5°, after at least a year's local ageing.

BIANCO di CUSTOZA (11°) Better known for the holiday villas of Verona's upper crust, and better still for the two Austrian victories, in 1848 and 1866, over Sardinian-Piedmontese armies in the wars of the Risorgimento, Custoza yields from its hillside vineyards a charming white wine. Made from rather more Trebbiano than Garganega grapes, and more like the Gavi wines of Piedmont (see chapter 4) than its fellow-Venetian Soave. Good with local lake and river fish, but there is little of it, and less still of the *spumante* version.

BREGANZE One *denominazione* for three whites: Breganze-Pinot Bianco and Breganze-Vespaiolo, from the grapes named (both 11·5°), and Breganze Bianco (11°), from Tocai Italiano; and three reds: Breganze-Pinot Nero and Breganze-Cabernet (both 11·5°), and Breganze Rosso (11°), from Merlot. From the hills north of Vicenza, a district noted also for its *grappa** and its asparagus, and largely from big new co-operatives.

Only the Bianco and the Rosso, both to be drunk young, are produced in any quantity, but the Cabernet, hard to find save locally, is regarded as the best.

COLLI BERICI Another blanket *denominazione*, this time for no fewer than seven wines from the hills south of Vicenza. There is three times as much Colli Berici-Garganega (10·5°) as the other three whites put together, from Tocai Italico, Sauvignon and Pinot Bianco respectively (all 11°). It is pleasant enough, not especially fragrant, but with an appetizing bitter-almond finish.

Of the reds (all 11°), there is twice as much Merlot as of the Tocai Rosso and the Cabernet put together. They are all lightish, rather astringent, and do not seem to mellow with age.

COLLI EUGANEI From another hilly district south of the Colli Berici – a dry Colli Euganei Bianco and a sweet white (both 10·5°), and a great deal more red (11°), from a blend in which Merlot predominates. The dry white is a good enough local wine, chiefly from the Garganego; the sweet is a typically scented Moscato; and the red is perhaps a cut above its neighbours from the Berici. All three can be made *spumante*, but I have yet to come across any sparkler from here, and doubt if much is made, or worth making.

GAMBELLARA (11°) Only a small amount is made of this dry white wine that is virtually a Soave (see below), being made from the same grapes in a next-door district; it is a little stronger. There is a *superiore* (11·5°), a sweetish Recioto (see under Soave and Valpolicella, below), a *spumante* and a richly sweet *vin santo* (14°) (see Appendix 1).

MONTELLO COLLI ASOLANI The hills at the northern edge of the plain of the Po 'seem to chase one another', according to the region's handbook on its wines, 'in the slow movement of a gigantic

* Grappa is the Italian equivalent of the French *marc*, a strong, colourless spirit distilled from the pips, skins and stalks of grapes left after they have been pressed for wine. But the district is called Grappa – one of its main towns, noted for its distillery, is Bassano del Grappa – not after the spirit but after Monte Grappa, the six thousand-foot stronghold held by the Italians against the Austrians during the Caporetto campaign of 1917-18.

green wave'. From this lovely, little-visited countryside come – as well as the mushrooms it is famous for – three wines each entitled to the overall *denominazione*.

There is five times as much Merlot (10·5°) as of the Cabernet (11°). As might be expected, the Merlot is the blander, the Cabernet firmer and with something of a herby tang. After two years' ageing, one of which must be in wood, and with an extra half-degree alcoholic strength, each may style itself *superiore*.

The production here of Prosecco, still and sparkling, is tiny compared with that of Prosecco di Conegliano-Valdobbiadene (see below) but its characteristics are the same.

PIAVE or VINI del PIAVE As usual, the Merlot is more plentiful than the Cabernet; each similar to its Montello counterpart (see above), save that the Piave wines are each half a degree stronger and that instead of the *superiore* qualification, the Merlot may be described as *vecchio* and the Cabernet as *riserva*.

There are also two whites, Tocai and Verduzzo, both 10·5°. (See chapter 8 for characteristics.)

PRAMAGGIORE, CABERNET di (11·5°)
PRAMAGGIORE, MERLOT di (11·5°) From the eastern extremity of the Veneto; this wine-growing district straddles the Veneto-Friuli border.

Ninety per cent Merlot, 10 per cent Cabernet, and vice-versa, are the proportions; as in all northern Italy, there is more Merlot than Cabernet. After ageing two years and reaching 12° the Merlot can be styled *riserva*; the Cabernet needs three years. As in the Médoc, where both are 'classic' grapes, the Merlot makes a softer wine than the Cabernet, whereas the Cabernet is harder and ages better. The Merlot does better in Italy than in France which, no doubt, is why more is produced, but the Cabernet *riserva* is more highly regarded than the Merlot. I can recommend both.

PROSECCO di CONEGLIANO-VALDOBBIADENE The two place-names may be hyphenated, as here, or each used separately. The Prosecco is the main grape for most of the Veneto's whites, but it is only here between the two small towns, in a vine and orchard-clad district south of Vittorio Veneto, that it is given a *denominazione* of its own. (Conegliano is a notable wine town, with a long-established Experimental Station for Viticulture and Oenology, co-operatives, cooperages, and other ancillary establishments.)

The *denominazione* covers a dry, an *amabile*, a *dolce* and a *frizzante* version (all 10·5°), and a *spumante* (11°) – both these last being dry. Wine from grapes harvested in a particularly respected district of Valdobbiadene, and reaching 11·5°, may add to its *denominazione* the qualification, *Superiore di Cartizze*.

The still wines are much like any others; it is the dry sparkler that merits attention. A little is made by the *méthode champenoise* (some by a co-operative, of a quality that commands and deserves high prices) but most by the *Charmat* or *cuve close* which, though lacking the prestige of *champenoise*, does preserve the fragrance of the grape, as the producers of Asti (see chapter 4) maintain. For the sparkling, made by whatever method, the law permits up to 25 per cent Pinot instead of the 15 per cent permitted to the still and *frizzante* wines.

SOAVE (10·5°) Not only the best-known but also the most plentiful of all Italian D.O.C. dry white wines, grown on the hillsides around the walled hilltop town of Soave, between Verona and Vicenza. Made largely from the Garganega grape but with up to 30 per cent of Trebbiano Toscana and Trebbiano di Soave, so long as there is no more than 15 per cent of the former. Wine made in the original heartland of the region may add *classico* to its *denominazione*, and a wine at least six months old, and reaching 11·5°, *superiore*.

When so much wine is produced by so many different firms – private and co-operative – quality must vary but, although some is undoubtedly better than others, I have never had a bad Soave – and I write as one who, over the past thirty-five years, has eaten a vast amount of fish in Venice, the Italian city I know best, almost invariably accompanied by Soave. (To say nothing of what I have drunk elsewhere.) At its best, a well-balanced wine, flowery to the nose, firm in flavour without being earthy; at its worst, the firmness is more pronounced than the floweriness and the wine is dull and characterless.

It is difficult, if not impossible, to discover how different producers make their Soave, but I am pretty certain that whereas some Soave, like other Italian whites, is fermented on the skins, for body and staying power, the best is made in the French way, quickly off the skins: the Garganega gives quite enough body, and staying power is hardly necessary in a wine that should be drunk young.

There is a sweet Recioto di Soave (14°) and a *liquoroso* (16°), made in the same way as the Recioto della Valpolicella (see below), entitled to the *denominazione*, as are the sparkling versions of the sweet and the dry Soave.

TOCAI di LISON (11·5°) Little is made of this dry white wine, made from at least 95 per cent Tocai (Tocai Friulano) grapes near the Pramaggiore district. The slightly bitter after-taste to the basic fruitiness – reminiscent, some say, of peach-kernels – goes well with the more savoury local fish dishes, such as *sfogi in saor* (otherwise, *sogliole in sapore*), a sort of sweet-sour, soused-fried, little sole. Tocai di Lison from the original central zone may be styled *classico*.

VALPOLICELLA (11°) If Soave is the best-known and easily the most plentiful white wine of the Veneto, Valpolicella is the best-known and most plentiful red; and if Soave is the best-known and most plentiful white D.O.C. wine in all Italy, Valpolicella ranks second only to Chianti among the D.O.C. reds. Indeed, if Valpolicella and Bardolino are considered together, there is more of these Veneto reds than there is of either Soave or Chianti. Made from the same grapes as Bardolino (see above), but grown inland from Garda and from heavier soil, Valpolicella is deeper in flavour but still a light wine, to be drunk young. Indeed, to compare it with Chianti is rather like comparing Beaujolais and Burgundy. Hemingway, habitué of Venice, describes it in *Across the River and into the Trees* as 'light, dry, red and genial, like the house of a brother with whom one gets on well'.

The *superiore* is fuller-bodied, with at least a year's ageing and 12°. The sweet Recioto della Valpolicella (14°) (cf. the Recioto di Soave) is made from the 'ears' of each bunch of grapes (*recioto* derives from *recie*, a corruption of *orecchie*, 'ears') – the outermost grapes, that is, that have enjoyed most sunshine and so yield the most sweetness; these are then part-dried to enhance the sweetness. This wine can be still or, rather like the Lambrusco of Emilia-Romagna (see chapter 9), become a sparkling or semi-sparkling sweet red. There is an even richer *liquoroso* Recioto.

If fermentation of a Recioto is fully completed, however, the result is a strong, full, dry wine, deep in colour and in flavour. The Recioto della Valpolicella Amarone ('bitter') is as hefty a red wine as any in northern Italy and more than able to stand up to the richest of stews and to *fegato alla veneziana* – thin flakes of calf's liver cooked briefly in oil and onions.

Valpolicella may call itself *classico* if it comes from the original centre of the wine-growing area, and hyphenate its name with that of Valpantena, a strictly demarcated and highly regarded district adjoining the *classico* area.

Other wines of the Veneto

BIANCO della VAL d'ALPONE
BIANCO VERONESE
DURELLO dei COLLI LESSINI (VERONESE e VICENTINO)
Not particularly distinguished white wines from the mainly red-wine region around Verona. The Durello *spumante* is spoken well of.

FRIULARO PADOVANO A light, rather sharp red, made inland from Chioggia, from a grape said to have come originally from Friuli, believed by some to be the same as the Raboso (see below).

PINOT GRIGIO del VENETO The grape is grown widely all over northern Italy, especially in the three Venetos: Veneto itself, Trentino-Alto Adige, and Friuli-Venezia Giulia. There is an ubiquitous 'Pinot Grigio delle Tre Venezie' that is not D.O.C. Nor is this; those of the other two regions are.

PROSECCO della MARCA TREVIGIANA A new relative of the D.O.C. Prosecco (see above) and worth considering.

RABOCO della MARCA TREVIGIANA Very dry, with a herby scent and taste, not unlike the Friularo (see above).

RIESLING del VENETO White wine, from the Riesling Italico, grown widely through the region but, like the Pinot Grigio, not so distinguished here as that from Trentino-Alto Adige and Friuli-Venezia Giulia.

ROSSO della VAL TRAMIGNA Small peasant production of a traditional wine, from much the same grapes as Valpolicella, and found only, so far as I know, in its own small district, not far from the more famous Veronese wines.

TORCOLATO di BREGANZE A sweet golden dessert wine from the Breganze district – in effect, a Breganze Bianco *dolce*.

VAL d'ILLASI A good deal of white, not much red, from near Verona, similar to, but not the equal of, Soave and Valpolicella.

VENEGAZZU Without any *denominazione* – not even listed in the Paldetto *Guida* as a *vino da tavola con indicazione* – because from grapes not regarded as 'classic' in the region, yet well enough known in 1973 to be listed in Giuseppe Coria's encyclopaedia, this is one of Italy's great wines. Made from a classic Bordeaux blend of Cabernet Sauvignon, Cabernet Franc, Malbec and Merlot, it is not unworthy to be ranked with fine clarets, and needs similar, though not perhaps quite so much, bottle-age. There is a good white, too, but it is the red that is keenly sought after by the grandest restaurants and the most knowledgeable amateurs.

Chapter 8

Friuli-Venezia Giulia

FRIULI-VENEZIA GIULIA did not become a region of Italy until 1963. First, dispute with Yugoslavia over Trieste had to be settled; there then followed long constitutional debates about how best to weld together, and give a measure of autonomy to, a region artifically made up of the wholly Italian agricultural province of Friuli, centred on Udine, and the industrial, commercial, shipyard-working fragment, from Gorizia to Trieste, left to Italy after much of the old Venezia-Giulia had passed to Yugoslavia – a fragment where, to some small extent still, Slav and Germanic cultural influences met and mingled.

Political instability meant that the region was slower than others, such as Sicily and Sardinia, in committing itself to improved wine-growing and wine-making; and it was not until the middle 1960s that, as a recent issue (April 1981) of *Which? Wine Monthly* pointed out, the E.E.C. and the Italian government (as well, one must add, as the regional government) 'pumped funds into Friulian viticulture, with an emphasis on new grape varieties and complete refurbishment of traditional vineyard areas' and 'the present quality-orientated industry began to grow'. This development has been controlled by a particularly efficient regional viticultural centre, helped by experimental establishments at Conegliano (see under Veneto), Udine and Gorizia.

The late start gave an opportunity to simplify D.O.C. regulations, much simpler and clearer here than in any of Italy's other nineteen regions. There are six *denominazioni*, each for a geographical zone. Within each zone, wines are classified according to specified grape varieties; although some varieties carry a *denominazione* in all six zones, others are entitled to it only in certain of them. They must bear varietal labels, and 90 per cent of the grapes used must be of the variety named.

75

The following lists, therefore, follow a pattern different from those in other chapters of this book: first, the D.O.C. zones, then the varieties of grape.

Before that, a brief mention of the region's cuisine – a mélange of Italian, Austro-Hungarian and Slav traditions, so that one may get as good goulashes, schnitzels, strudels and liver-dumplings here as in their native countries, as well as the pastas of southern Italy and the polentas and risotti of the north. Especially, though, the best of all raw hams, that of San Daniele near Udine, with a *denominazione* of its own, each ham carrying its seal of authenticity.

Here, then, the wines to match this array of different dishes.

D.O.C. wines of Friuli-Venezia Giulia

THE ZONES

AQUILEIA Coastal plain, south of Udine, west of Isonzo, with a particularly good co-operative, its wines brand-named Molin di Ponte. Most of its wines are red, and mostly Merlot. Given D.O.C. status as recently as 1975, along with Latisana, its neighbour to the west (see below).

COLLIO GORIZIANO (or COLLIO, simply) This, on the other hand, the smallest but perhaps the most distinguished of the zones, was the first to be given its D.O.C., in 1968. It is a gently hilly district, west of Gorizia; the altitude of the vineyards, though modest, combines with the cooling sea breezes to provide a micro-climate that seems especially suitable for white wines, perhaps the best of the region. More individual growers and fewer co-operatives here than in Aquileia.

COLLI ORIENTALI del FRIULI Another hilly zone, to the east, as the name indicates, of Collio Goriziano, along the frontier with Yugoslavia, north of Gorizia. Notable especially for its Picolit (see below).

GRAVE del FRIULI The biggest of the region's six zones – the name, like that of the French Graves, indicates gravelly soil, in this case the alluvial plain below the Julian Alps in the north of the region. The Merlot thrives here, and the zone is famous for its great vine nursery at Rauscedo.

ISONZO Between Collio Goriziano and the sea, along the Isonzo river, scene of much fighting in the First World War. A small zone, similar in size and in micro-climate, being largely coastal plain, to Aquileia and Latisana, its wines are similar, if usually a little lighter and softer.

LATISANA So near geographically, climatically and in character, to Aquileia (see above) that it was thought at one time that they would form one zone.

THE GRAPE VARIETIES

CABERNET Not the most heavily but, geographically, the most widely cultivated variety of the region, D.O.C. in all six zones. May be either Cabernet Franc or Cabernet Sauvignon, or a blend of both, which leads to varying styles in the region. Both are French varieties, 'noble' in Bordeaux, though Cabernet Franc is relatively little used there, many of the great clarets being largely – some almost entirely – Cabernet Sauvignon, 'the grape on which claret's reputation is founded', as Edmund Penning-Rowsell points out in his classic *The Wines of Bordeaux*. The Cabernet Franc, like the Merlot, seems to do better in Italy than in its native France.

    Aquileia Cabernet (11·5°) May be either the Franc or the Sauvignon, or a blend. Not so roundly satisfying as the zone's Merlot (of which there is twice as much), but easy to drink and sweet-smelling – some detect a smell as of new-mown grass.

    Colli Orientali Cabernet (12°) Usually, but not necessarily, Cabernet Franc; fuller in colour, scent and strength than that of Aquileia (above), but only a quarter as much produced as of the Merlot. This is the only zone with a Cabernet *riserva*, which calls for two years' ageing.

    Collio (or Collio Goriziano) Cabernet (12°) This *denominazione* calls for Cabernet Franc alone; not so full in colour as some, but stronger than others in alcohol.

    Grave del Friuli Cabernet (11·5°) Softer and lighter than that of other zones, save Isonzo, and only one-fifth as much produced as of the zone's Merlot.

    Isonzo Cabernet (11°) Lightest and softest of all the zone's Cabernets and to some, therefore, the most attractive.

    Latisana Cabernet (11·5°) Most people – and I am one of them – find this indistinguishable from the Cabernet of Aquileia.

MALVASIA D.O.C. in two zones – Collio (11·5°) and Isonzo (10·5°). A golden white wine, in Isonzo sometimes called Malvasia Istriana, as this is the Istrian peninsula. Full in flavour and, according to some, suitable for the richer fish dishes, though others will find it not so clean and crisp as they feel a white wine should be. Indeed, Burton Anderson has found in some 'an aromatic lushness'.

MERLOT Ask for a red D.O.C. wine in Friuli-Venezia Giulia and the odds are somewhere between five and ten to one that you will be offered a Merlot – and the odds are better than that that you will be pleased with it. The Merlot is the grape that gives softness and delicacy to the great clarets – more particularly in St Emilion and Pomerol (notably in that great wine, Pétrus) and, to a lesser but important extent, in the Médoc (Lafite is a fine example).

More resistant to disease in Italy than in Bordeaux, it makes a quick-maturing wine, which helps to keep prices down. Styles vary a little between the zones, but a Friuli-Venezia Giulia Merlot, fresh, fruity and well-rounded, is one of Italy's best reds for consistency and value. It is D.O.C. in all zones, the dominant red in all of them, and it must always be 100 per cent varietal – no blending permitted.

It varies so little throughout the region that all that needs to be said here about the six zones is that only in the Colli Orientali is Merlot (like the same zone's Cabernet) permitted to be styled *riserva* after two years' ageing before bottling; and that here and in Collio Goriziano it must reach 12°, whereas in Isonzo it is only 10·5° – quite a difference, though it is not so different in the mouth. The Grave Merlot (11°) is perhaps the most highly esteemed, but I have never tasted an unsatisfactory Merlot from anywhere in the region.

PICOLIT (15°) D.O.C. only in Colli Orientali, and very little of it even there (a very little is grown, non-D.O.C., in the Isonzo zone and elsewhere in northern Italy). Soft, sweetish to fully sweet, and strong, it was much admired abroad in Victorian times, and even compared to Yquem, before its grape fell victim to the disease of floral abortion and virtually disappeared. I think that its sweetness derives partly from semi-dried grapes. It is much more delicate and less cloying than most sweet white wines and, though certainly no rival to Yquem, might perhaps be regarded as the Yquem of Italy – which is not quite the same thing. Some – myself not among them – like it not only with fruit and puddings but (as some Bordelais like their Sauternes) with rich liver pâtés and even with strong cheese, such as Gorgonzola.

PINOT BIANCO This is not, as is sometimes supposed, the grape of white burgundy, which is the Chardonnay – there is no such thing as a Pinot-Chardonnay* – but the Clevner of Alsace. It is D.O.C. in all six zones and varies little, save that in Collio Goriziano and Colli Orientali it must reach 12°; in Grave, Aquileia, and Latisana 11·5°; and in Isonzo 11°. It is usually yellowish as white wines go, and sometimes seems to have a touch of an Alsatian scent and savour about it. Not so highly regarded among the region's whites as the Pinot Grigio and the Tocai.

PINOT GRIGIO Also a French grape – it makes the Pinot Gris, or Tokay, of Alsace. Also D.O.C. in all six zones, it varies more widely than the Pinot Bianco does because of different house styles – some producers leave the must on the skins much longer than others do, resulting in a more opulent wine. Generally speaking, though, it is fuller than the Pinot Bianco, deeper in colour, richer on the nose, and longer-lived, very like the Rülander of the Alto Adige (see chapter 6). This is also a name sometimes used in Alsace for the Pinot Gris. Goes with many rich dishes that might otherwise call for a red-wine accompaniment. In Collio Goriziano 12·5°; in Colli Orientali 12°; in the other zones 11°. That of Isonzo is said by many locals to be especially good.

PINOT NERO Otherwise the Borgogna Rossa, the Pinot Noir of Burgundy. D.O.C. only in Collio Goriziano (12·5°) and Colli Orientali (12°); very little produced in either zone. In the Orientale it can become a *riserva* after two years' ageing. It is not in the same class as the region's Merlot or Cabernet, and certainly not to be compared to what the French make of the grape.

REFOSCO There are three sub-varieties of this grape, which is native to the region and was not, as were most of the other red varieties, introduced after the phylloxera had passed – Refosco del Peduncolo Rosso, Refosco Friuliano, also known as Refosco Nostrano, and Terrano, which is a Refosco not entitled to the *denominazione*.

The two others are D.O.C. in four zones. In Colli Orientali the D.O.C. Refosco may be made from either the Nostrano or the Peduncolo, must reach 12°, and becomes a *riserva* with two years' ageing. In Grava and Aquileia it must be made from the Peduncolo and reach 11°. The same strength must be reached in Latisana, where

* See Arlott and Fielden, *Burgundy: Vines and Wines*, London, 1976, chapter 2.

79

both types may be used, separately or together.

Refosco is generally a hearty, full, dry red wine. It pays for ageing; I think a *riserva* from the Orientale would be a rewarding drink with a rich stew on a cold Friuli evening.

RIBOLLA (12°) A lightly flavoured, strongish, faintly sweet white wine, D.O.C. only in the Colli Orientali (though the grape is a component of the blend called simply Collio Bianco; see entry at the end of this chapter). Even here, little is produced. Fair enough as an accompaniment to local freshwater fish, but I understand why the region's growers would rather have it in a blend than on its own.

RIESLING ITALICO (12°) The 'foreign' or Welschriesling, D.O.C. only in Collio Goriziano, where it makes a rather drier but also rather coarser wine than the Renano (below). More akin to the Yugoslav rieslings than to those of Germany.

RIESLING RENANO The Rhine or German riesling is D.O.C. in Colli Orientali (12°) and Isonzo (11°), and in both zones must be 100 per cent varietal. In Aquileia 10 per cent of other varieties is permitted. Quality varies; I have not come across a Rhine riesling of the region that is in the same class as typical examples from Germany or Alsace – and none so good as the best of the Alto Adige. I have heard, though, of exceptional bottles, and such would be worth a certain amount of experimental tasting.

SAUVIGNON Another grape, like the Cabernet, the Merlot, and the various Pinots, that is of French origin – the grape of the great dry Loires and the sweet Sauternes among others, and now the greatest of the California whites. It is D.O.C. in three zones – Colli Orientali (12°), Collio Goriziano (12·5°), and Isonzo (11°). This is the best region in Italy for the Sauvignon – especially, perhaps, in the Isonzo zone, where it shows something of the flowery scent and the appetizingly crisp finish found in the great whites of the Loire.

TOCAI First of all the white grapes of the region in volume, the Tocai covers a quarter of the region's area under vines (the red Merlot covers about half), and its wine is D.O.C. in all zones. Some say that it has no connection with the Tokay of Hungary, some that it came from there in the eleventh century. However that may be, if it was not Italian-born, it is now completely assimilated, and its wine bears no resemblance to that of Hungary. It varies considerably, both between zones and between producers, but in general it is dry and full, with a bitter finish after a lemony first taste in the mouth.

In Collio Goriziano and Colli Orientali it must reach 12°; in Aquileia, Latisana and Isonzo (where not so much is grown) 11°, and 11° also in Grave, where nearly as much is grown as in all five other zones put together.

TRAMINER The Traminer of Germany and Alsace is said to have come originally from around the Tyrolean village of Tramin (Termeno) (see under Alto Adige Traminer, chapter 6), and it is something of a speciality in that part of Italy. Here, it is D.O.C. only in two of the region's zones – Collio Goriziano (12°) and Isonzo (11°), in both of which it becomes Traminer Aromatico, which corresponds to the German and Alsatian Gewürztraminer ('spicy Traminer'). Little is made in either zone, and although it has something of the big bouquet and the full flavour of its cousins elsewhere, I do not see its developing in Friuli-Venezia Giulia at the expense of the region's better-known whites.

VERDUZZO One *denominazione* covers two kinds of white wine made from the Verduzzo grape. One is the Verduzzo Friuliano, which one authority credits with a 'light, even salty dryness', another (who must have a highly developed sense of smell) with 'hints of sweet almonds, acacia and peach in its aroma', while still acknowledging it as dry. The other wine from the grape is undoubtedly sweet: the Verduzzo di Ramandolo, made partly from semi-dried grapes, richly scented, and sometimes *frizzante*.

The latter is named after a commune in the north of the Colli Orientali – the only zone to include the Ramandalo in its *denominazione* along with the dry Verduzzo Friuliano.

Note: the only D.O.C. wine of the region that is not a varietal is the Collio Bianco (or Collio Goriziano Bianco) (11°), made from a blend of about half Ribolla Gialla, the rest Malvasia Istriana and Tocai Italico. Very light, sometimes with a slight prickle, not much of it, and not much to say to nose or palate. I am surprised that it was awarded D.O.C. status.

Other wines of Friuli-Venezia Giulia

FRANCONIA di CORNO di ROSAZZO Red wine from the Franconia grape, the origins of which are obscure, produced in small quantities in the Colli Orientale. It has not come my way, so I have no reason to dispute the verdict of the magazine *Italian Wines and Spirits* (February 1981) that it is 'a fine minor wine' – to be drunk young, I gather, when it is sometimes *frizzante*.

MARZEMINO di CASARSA Small quantities are produced of this lightish red wine – though nothing like so much as the wine from the same grape in Trentino-Alto Adige (see chapter 6), which it resembles.

PIGNOLO di PREPOTTO Another light red wine, made to be drunk young, produced on a smallish scale around Albana di Prepotto in the Colli Orientale.

PINOT NERO della PROVINCIA di UDINE The same wine as the D.O.C. Pinot Nero (see above), but made outside the area in which it is entitled to the *denominazione*.

PUCINO del CARSO A white wine grown in the Carso Hills, north-east of Trieste, along the Yugoslav frontier. I doubt whether any is to be found outside Trieste save at the vineyard gates of small producers.

SAUVIGNON Such as is grown outside the D.O.C. areas: see under the D.O.C. Sauvignon.

SCHIOPPETTINO di PREPOTTO Red from the same district as the Pignolo (above), but more full-bodied. Also known as Ribolla Nera and Pocalza.

TAZZELENGHE del FRIULI or TAZZALENA Red, said to be similar to the D.O.C. Refosco (above) but from an indigenous grape, grown in small quantities near Udine.

TERRANO del CARSO Red wine from a grape long established along the Istrian and Dalmatian coasts, on both sides of the Italian-Yugoslav frontier, and possibly a sort of Refosco (see above). Low in alcohol, light, with a blossomy scent, and *frizzante* when very young. I have enjoyed it in Trieste restaurants, some of which, I have heard it whispered, smuggle it in from Yugoslavia.

Note: there are also non-D.O.C. versions of the Traminer, the Malvasia and the Refosco (see under D.O.C. wines of Friuli-Venezia Giulia) and the Prosecco (see chapter 7.

Chapter 9

Emilia-Romagna

THE great cities of this region are Parma, noted for Parma hams and Parmesan cheese; Ferrara, which has given its name to the crustiest of Italian loaves – available, much to this author's delight, in a few at any rate of Soho's Italian shops – the *ferravese*; Modena, home of *zampone*, the sausage-stuffed pig's trotter; and Bologna *la grassa*, 'Bologna the fat', after which great university city some sorts of sausage come to be called 'polony', and whence come, traditionally, Italy's greatest cooks. The country's best restaurants cluster as closely around Bologna and Modena as do those of France around Lyons and Dijon. It has been said that an Emilian eats as much in a day as a Roman in a week and a Genoese (the Aberdonian of Italy) in a month: this is the belly of Italy.

Verdi, a notable lover of good food and wine, came from these parts, and Rossini, born in Pesaro, just over the border with the Marche, made his home in Bologna, where he is regarded as a true Bolognese for his love of good living – consider the richness of a *tournedos Rossini*, with its truffles, *pâté de foie gras*, butter and madeira. This is Don Camillo's country, too – an indication not only of good, hearty eating but of good, hearty fun.

No wine of this region is so famous – or, at any rate, so highly regarded – as its ham, its sausages and its cheese, or as the greatest wines of neighbouring Tuscany, but I am not the only one to maintain that the dry version of the controversial Lambrusco is just the red wine to 'cut' the richness of the best-known pork and ham dishes of Bologna and Modena – though there are regional wines, notably those from the Sangiovese grape of nearby Chianti, to placate those who prefer their red wines to be of a more conventional style.

For the fish dishes of the Adriatic coast, there are dry white wines from the Trebbiano grape and, with varying degrees of semi-sweetness, from the Albana, that will appeal, as resembling their own hocks, to the German sun-seekers who throng the holiday towns strung along the coast between Ravenna and Rimini.

D.O.C. wines of Emilia-Romagna

ALBANA di ROMAGNA There is a *secco* (12°) and an *amabile* (12·5°) version of this white wine of the region, and a sparkling version of each, made from the Albana grape. Alexis Lichine, in his great *Encyclopedia of Wines and Spirits*, finds 'a noticeably velvety quality' in Albana of good years, but I have not found any noticeable difference between vintages, nor any especially velvety quality. The *secco* is clean at the finish and never austerely dry, the *amabile* never lusciously sweet, the *spumante* neither here nor there. A useful white wine suitable, according to its dryness or sweetness, for fish or fruit and produced in usefully large quantities.

BIANCO di SCANDINO (10·5°) Also a dry and a fairly sweet, and a sparkling version of the semi-sweet (11°). There is not much made, and although it comes chiefly from the distinguished Sauvignon grape (known locally as the Spergola or Spergolina), there is not much to be said about it.

COLLI BOLOGNESI (di MONTE S. PIETRO or dei CASTELLI MEDIEVALI) That there are two alternative names is due to there being two rival *consorzi* of growers. What is much more confusing is that the generic *denominazione* covers no fewer than six wines, each of which must be made from at least 85 per cent of the varietal named:
    Barbera (11·5°) From the great grape of Piedmont (see chapter 4), and reasonably similar to that – at its best – sound, rather earthy, red wine. The young Colli Bolognesi Barbera, though, can be slightly *frizzante*, and this is true, too, of the other Colli wines. The Barbera is the only one of the six to be permitted to style itself *riserva* after three years in wood and reaching 12·5°.
    Bianco (11°) The only Colli Bolognesi wine not a varietal, and the lightest, which is no bad thing. Blended from Albana (see above) and Trebbiano grapes, the better bottles show more of the Albana than the Trebbiano in style.
    Merlot (11·5°) So little is produced that I have never come across

any, and cannot understand how it came by its *denominazione*. It is said by those who know to be more elegant and smoother than the Barbera.

Pinot Bianco (12°) The *denominazione* covers an *abboccato* as well as a dry version. The sweetish one is fairly commonplace, the dry not so delicate as the Sauvignon, but sound and sturdy.

Riesling Italico (12°) Not so fragrant as some north Italian wines purportedly from the same grape. Some consider that is is not, strictly speaking, an Italian riesling, but the local descendant of the Rhine riesling brought many generations ago from Germany itself. Lacks the balanced character of the region's Sauvignon.

Sauvignon (12°) High in alcohol for a white wine of this type. Similar to that of Emilia-Romagna (see chapter 9), and one of the best whites of the region.

GUTTURNIO dei COLLI PIACENTINI (12°) A bright, clear red, from Barbera and Bonarda grapes from around Piacenza. It was here that, a century ago, a particularly fine Roman *gutturnium*, or drinking cup, was found: the local red wine has been named after it. Usually light and fruity, with an underlying sweetness, of the same refreshing type as the light reds of Lake Garda (see under the Veneto).

LAMBRUSCO I once quoted two distinguished American gastronomes as agreeing that this was 'as nearly undrinkable as a well-known wine could be', whereas the equally distinguished Elizabeth David had said that 'it sounds so dubious and is in fact delicious'. I added that I was with Elizabeth David and the Bolognesi in this matter.

Since then, Lambrusco has burst upon the U.S. market, as explosively as Lancers there and Mateus Rosé here. Most, I gather, is sweet and much more bubbly than the traditional Lambrusco, the considerable froth of which soon subsides into a modest prickle. When I first came across it, most Lambrusco was dry, and the Bolognesi themselves turned up their noses at what they called Lambruscola, and made so much money out of, from the less sophisticated Americans.

Now, more sweet wine is being drunk by the Bolognesi, though the dry, even slightly bitter wine, made by the traditional method of fermentation in bottle, still appeals to the *cognoscenti*, who claim, not that this is a great wine, but that it is special to the region, and the best wine to 'cut' the fattiness of its rich pork dishes. To my mind, they are right.

There are four D.O.C. Lambruschi; the Sorbara from Modena is usually considered the best:

Lambrusco di Sorbara (11°)

Lambrusco Grasparossa di Castelvetro (9·5°) The Grasparossa is a sub-variety of the grape.

Lambrusco Reggiano

Lambrusco Salamino di S. Croce (11°) Another sub-variety.

In each case, there is a dry and a sweet, and the *denominazione* is permitted to wines from outside the prescribed zone so long as all other regulations are observed (grape variety, production per hectare, alcoholic strength and so on) and so long as the wine is labelled *vinificato fuori zona*.

MONTEROSSO VAL d'ARDA (11°) It is the *monte* that is *rosso*, not the wine, from a blend of local white grapes: sometimes still, sometimes sparkling, sometimes sweet, sometimes dry – though always with a touch of sweetness. A young wine for young people, especially if they like frogs' legs – Bruno Roncarati considers them the ideal accompaniment.

SANGIOVESE di ROMAGNA (11·5°) The classic Chianti grape is grown widely throughout the region, so there is plenty to go with hearty Bolognese meat dishes. I cannot agree with Felice Cùnsolo that it has more personality than Chianti, but it is better made than when I first came across it, before D.O.C. took effect.

TREBBIANINO VAL TREBBIA (11°) From the Trebbia valley, south of Piacenza, said to have given its name to the Trebbiano, one of north and central Italy's most important white wine grape. Trebbianino, though, is made from a blend, with not much Trebbiano – hence a name that means 'little Trebbiano'. A modest wine, little known outside its own area, pleasant enough when young, when it often shows a youthful prickle.

TREBBIANO di ROMAGNA (11°) This, on the other hand, is entirely from the named grape, and there is six or seven times as much as there is of the Trebbianino; it is the region's white equivalent of the Sangiovese – a sound, well-made, reliable wine to go with local dishes, if not so elegant as the Trebbiano of Orvieto (see chapter 11). There is a *spumante* version, dry, sweet or semi-sweet, but other regions do better ones.

Other wines of Emilia-Romagna

BIANCO ROMAGNOLO White wine of the region, mostly from the Albana or Trebbiano or both; can be taken seriously when offered in good restaurants, but one of the D.O.C. whites will normally show more style.

BIANCO VAL TIDONE Blend of Malvasia, Ortugo and Moscato with Trebbiano, with rather more substance than the better-known Bianco Romagnolo (above).

BONARDA di ZIANO Sweetish red from the Bonarda grape of the Oltrepò.

CANINA della PROVINCIA di RAVENNA Red, from an indigenous grape near the coast, where it is mostly to be found.

FORTANA PARMENSE Sort of local Lambrusco from around Parma.

LANCELOTTA della PROVINCIA di REGGIO EMILIA Much the same sort of thing as Fortana (above), said to be much appreciated by Swiss importers.

MONTUNO del RENO Dry, white wine, more usually *frizzante* than still. Rather full and hard.

ROSSO ROMAGNOLO Apart from the colour, much the same can be said of this as of the *Bianco* (above).

Chapter 10

Tuscany

THE Tuscan landscape and the light that illumines it are familiar to millions of men and women who have never set foot in Italy, but who know the colour and the contours, the hills and the poplars – the very look of the people – from two and a half centuries of genius: from the paintings of Giotto and Leonardo, Botticelli and Uccello, Fra Angelico and Michelangelo.

Florence was the centre and capital of the school of painting to which these life-enhancing artists belonged, and Florence is the centre and capital of a wine-growing district similarly known by name not only to people who have never trodden Italian soil but to people who have never tasted a glass of wine in their lives: who has not heard of Chianti?

Chianti – and, because of Chianti, Tuscany – hold a special place in any book about Italian wine. Not because it is the *best* Italian wine. I do not think it is: it is a great wine, undoubtedly, but there are others that could claim a higher rank in any Debrett or Almanach de Gotha of the wines of Italy. But it is the greatest D.O.C. district in the country, both in area – a million acres or so, roughly in and around the triangle bounded by the ancient cities of Florence, Arezzo and Siena – and in production: 100 million litres of D.O.C. wine a year, let alone good wine not accorded the *denominazione*.

Nor is Chianti important only because of area and bulk. It is fifty years since the then leading growers of Chianti persuaded the Italian government of the time to delimit the area to which the term 'Chianti Classico' could be applied, thus setting a pattern for the protection of the names and styles of Italian wines that has developed into the strict D.O.C. regulations of our own time.

It seems a strange anomaly that, this being so, Chianti was not first in the list of *denominazioni* granted in 1966 under the terms of the then new Italian wine law. This was because differences of opinion as to standards and zones between the various *consorzi* of growers delayed application for more than a year. But it is worth noting that it is another Tuscan wine that heads the list – the white Vernaccia di San Gimignano – and that another white, the Bianco di Pitigliano, and the Brunello di Montalcino, which many regard as the greatest red wine of Italy, and some as one of the greatest in Europe, were among the first eight given their accolade, in May 1966. This is a reminder that there are Tuscan wines other than Chianti – white wines to accompany the *cacciucco*, a sort of Tuscan *bouillabaisse*, the fried red mullet and the baby eels of Livorno and Pisa, as well as one of the noblest of red wines to complement what is undoubtedly the noblest of all beefsteaks, the formidable *bistecca fiorentina*, three-quarters of a kilo, two fingers thick, of baby beef, as well as the Chianti countryside's rich stews of hare and wild boar.

This is not only bottle-and-glass country but, like Emilia-Romagna, knife-and-fork country.

D.O.C. wines of Tuscany

BIANCO della VALDINIEVOLE (11°) Clear, light, dry white wine from the Trebbiano grape produced in the district around the fashionable spa town of Montecatini, where the rich, diet-conscious patients must find it an agreeable accompaniment to their obligatory light meals. There is also a limited production of a dry (12°), semi-sweet (13°) and sweet (14°) *vin santo* (see Appendix 1) from the same grapes, semi-dried, and aged for at least three years. The fully sweet, to my mind, is more acceptable as a dessert wine than either of the other two as aperitifs.

BIANCO di PITIGLIANO (11·5°) Another white chiefly from the Trebbiano grape, but from the bleak countryside in the south of Tuscany, on the boundary with Umbria. It is dry and delicate, perhaps because of the volcanic soil, and quite the most plentiful of the Tuscan D.O.C. whites. Named after the little town of Pitigliano, in the centre of the wine-growing district, where most of the wine is made in two big co-operatives. The town has been something of a Jewish centre since the sixteenth century and is sometimes known as *la piccola Gerusalemme*; the Chief Rabbi of Livorno supervises the production of a *kosher* Pitigliano wine for the Passover.

BIANCO PISANO di S. TORPE Yet another Tuscan Trebbiano, this one from the Pisa part of the Chianti zone; its promotion to D.O.C. status is so recent at the time of writing that no details of strength and output are yet available. But it has long had a reputation as an especially appetizing dry wine with a fruity acidity.

BIANCO VERGINE VAL di CHIANA (11°) Trebbiano yet again, but *vergine* because it is fermented off skins, pips and stalks. This gives great delicacy; the wine is dry but with a hint of sweetness because of the consequent lack of tannin. One of the most interesting whites of the region.

BRUNELLO di MONTALCINO (12·5°) One of the greatest – many whose opinions I respect state positively, the greatest – of all Italian reds, made from the Brunello grape, a close relative of Chianti's Sangiovese, in a small area around Montalcino, just to the south of the Chianti zone. Much esteemed, much sought after and therefore, of course, expensive. Although production is small at present, a good deal of investment money – much of it American – is being poured in, and we can expect more planting within the permitted area, and much more Brunello.

A 1975, tasted in 1981, was described as 'chewy, dry, with a lot of tannin: some fruit, very austere', which suggests that it needed longer still in bottle, though colour at the rim was already showing age.

Meanwhile, this strong, warm, deep red wine has to be aged in wood for four years before it may be sold – five years for a *riserva* – is said to be the longest-lived of all unfortified wines (Veronelli says that fifty years in bottle is not too much), and should be decanted as much as twenty-four hours before serving.

CARMIGNANO (12·5°) A Chianti, the growers of which asked, and were permitted, to revert to the name they had borne, and been proud of, in the eighteenth century. To justify the differentiation, the blend is now very slightly different in proportion from that of Chianti,* but even an expert would be hard put to it to tell the difference; this is a soft, fragrant, most friendly red wine.

May not be sold until after two years' ageing in oak or chestnut-

---

* It would appear that up to 10 per cent of Cabernet is permitted (whether Sauvignon or Franc I do not know) which seems odd in the light of the explanation given for the ineligibility of Sassicaia and Timignano (see pp. 96-7). It may be that account is taken here of a long local tradition, which would not apply to the other wines, recently introduced.

wood, for three years from the St Michael's Day (29 September) after the vintage to be classed *riserva*.

CHIANTI One of the world's most famous dry red wines, produced in prodigious quantities from the inland hill country lying approximately in the triangle bounded by the ancient cities of Florence, Arezzo and Siena. Its composition – from 50 to 80 per cent Sangiovese, 10 to 30 per cent Canaiolo Nero, and 10 to 30 per cent Trebbiano and Malvasia – was hit upon as the result of a ballroom tiff.

Bettino, Baron Ricasoli, later the second prime minister of united Italy, was a stern and studious young nobleman when, in the 1830s, he took his young wife to a ball in Florence. When Anna was unwise enough to allow a young man to dance with her more often than the stiffly possessive Bettino thought proper, 'We must leave, my dear,' he said; called his carriage; and the two were driven south through the night to Brolio.

Brolio is the family seat, a grim lonely castle in the hills above Siena; they lived there for the next ten years, Anna devoting herself to her daughter, Bettino to the study of wine-growing and wine-making, trying new combinations of the region's traditional varieties of grape.

If Ricasoli did not invent Chianti, he certainly created the Chianti style we know today: all the growers of the region work within that general style which – although there are differences between one grower's wine and another's – is always recognizably Chianti.

There are two types of Chianti – wine to be drunk young, almost as soon as bottled, and wine meant for ageing, sometimes very considerable ageing. The fresh and fruity young wine – sometimes so young as even to be slightly *frizzante* – is put up in the traditional *fiasco*, its shape based on the goatskin wine bag that an Italian of the Middle Ages might have slung from his saddle-bow. It is traditional and picturesque, but it is suitable only for wine to be drunk young, for it cannot be laid down for maturing.

There was a time, before the now rigorous Italian wine law began to bite, when Chianti got a bad name abroad – largely because foreign wine shippers insisted on having their Chianti in the *fiasco*, because of its looks, and kept it too long.

The *fiasco* has become something of a problem. The marsh-grass which, when dried, becomes the straw for covering the flask, is now rare and expensive, as marshland is being drained and land reclaimed. The women who used to cover the flasks at home now go out to better paid work. (I have seen cheap and nasty flasks in cheap and nasty shops in Florence and Siena with plastic in place of the straw, and been glad to learn that the Italian authorities forbid their export.)

The paradox is that the proper straw-covered *fiasco* now costs four times as much as the claret-type bottle into which goes the more expensive wine. But this cheaper bottle is the one to look for if you are after the best – by which I mean the most mature – wines of the region. (The young wine is delicious drunk cool, like a Beaujolais.) Vintage dates mean little in themselves, for the Tuscan climate is more consistent than those of France and Germany, but they indicate age: for a Chianti *vecchio* the law requires at least two years' maturing, and for a *riserva* three. Most of the great Chianti houses give their best wines rather more.

They also give names of their own to their best wines, with 'Chianti' simply as a secondary qualification. Thus, the house of Ricasoli – presided over by the direct descendant of Bettino of the ballroom – styles its finest wine after the family seat, Brolio (not to be confused with the Piedmontese Barolo).

Confusion can be caused by the fact that some Chiantis bear a neck-label showing a black cockerel, some a naked cherub, some simply the firm's trademark. The cockerel and the cherub, though the badges of perfectly respectable voluntary bodies, do not indicate any sort of official recognition.

The Italian wine law gives its *denominazione* to two Chiantis only: the one made anywhere in the zone of inland Tuscany officially defined in 1963, and denominated simply Chianti (11·5°); and Chianti Classico (12°), from the heart of the region, the producers of which had formed themselves, forty years earlier, into a self-help consortium, pledged to maintain standards. Its badge is the *gallo nero*, the black cockerel.

Other producers, in areas surrounding the *classico*, have since formed themselves into a consortium of their own. The Chianti with a *putto* – a naked cherub – label, comes from between Florence and the *classico* zone, and some fine wines bear its badge. Some equally fine do not, just as firms entitled to join the black cockerel organization, such as Ricasoli, have opted out, arguing that the work once done by the consortium is now done disinterestedly by the wine law and that the consumer's best guarantee is a combination of the *denominazione* and the reputation of an old-established firm. Quite so, remembering that some of the best wines bear a cherub or a cockerel on their labels – and that some do not.

Chianti at its best – I am thinking now of the mature wine: to my mind, the younger wine in its *fiasco* is for picnics in the Tuscan countryside – is rich, fragrant and full, satisfying rather than subtle. Like most wines, it goes best with the characteristic dishes of its region – in Chianti country beefsteaks and game stews.

ELBA Very little red (12°) is made in the island – a sort of minor, but acceptable, local Chianti type. The more plentiful white (11°) is almost entirely of Trebbiano – called here Procanico – and a good wine with the excellent local fish dishes. The *spumante* may be *made* on the mainland so long as the wine itself comes from Elba.

MONTECARLO (11·5°) In this white wine, produced in small quantities near the coast, the dominant Trebbiano is blended with such classic French grapes as Sauvignon and Sémillon; its elegance shows at its best *nell'annata* – drunk within a year of its making.

MONTESCUDAIO (11·5°) Also from near the coast, a white and a red and a white *vin santo* (14°). The white, a typical Tuscan Trebbiano, is particularly light; the red is said to be like a rather light Chianti; and the *vin santo* is the usual rich dessert wine made from semi-dried grapes (see Appendix 1) – there is little of it.

MORELLINO di SCANSANO (11·5°) A red, chiefly Sangiovese, from the inland countryside near Pitigliano. It is perhaps a little drier than most typical Chiantis, and is not as distinguished among reds as is the Pitigliano (see above) among whites.

PARRINA (11·5°) From the southern end of the Tuscan coast near the Argentario peninsula, in what used to be the Maremma marshland, now reclaimed. Although the soil and micro-climate are so different from those of inland Tuscany, the red, from Sangiovese, and the white, from Trebbiano, are both typical Tuscan wines. But there is barely enough of either to do more than provide the hotels and restaurants of Porto Ercole and Porto Santo Stefano.

ROSSO delle COLLINE LUCCHESI (11·5°) This is in effect the red brother of the white Montecarlo (see above), grown in the mainly olive-growing hill country near Lucca. There is less of it than there is of the Montecarlo, and it is unlikely to be met with outside its own countryside – certainly not in the district that grows Chianti, to which it is similar – because it uses much the same blend of grapes – but inferior.

VERNACCIA di SAN GIMIGNANO (12°) The first name in the

list of *denominazioni* published after the passing of the Italian wine law. Although this may mean merely that its producers were the first to apply, or that there happened to be no minor problems to be solved, nevertheless it is a distinction, whether by chance or not, and this is an important, 'big' white wine that deserves it. Made from a local grape, Vernaccia, from around the self-consciously picturesque, many-towered Gimignano, it ages well and is a firmer, deeper-flavoured wine than many another Italian white. With a year's ageing in wood it can be styled *riserva* (but it can do with more than that in bottle). There is also a rich *liquoroso*, which shows nothing like the same distinction as the dry.

VINO (sometimes written as VIN, simply) NOBILE di MONTEPULCIANO (11·5°) Montepulciano is a small, pictur-esque town not unlike San Gimignano, but twice the size and half as famous. Its wine is made from much the same blend of grapes as Chianti, which it closely resembles. A fine red wine, well-balanced and smooth, it ages well. It must have at least two years in wood; with three years, it may be styled *riserva*, and with four, *riserva speciale*. I have not experimented, but suspect that age in bottle might do more for it than age in wood, and that the non-*riserva* with some ten years' bottle-age might be this splendid wine at its best. The word '*nobile*' derives from the history of the wine: it used to be made by the local nobility for sacramental use. A wine labelled simply 'Montepulciano' is one with no *denominazione*, and not governed by D.O.C. rules, though it might well be very acceptable.

Other wines of Tuscany

BIANCO della LUCCHESIA At the time of writing there is a move on foot to give this D.O.C. status as the white partner of Rosso delle Colline Lucchesi (see above), which means that it is much the same wine as Montecarlo (see above). It may well be that it is only parochial patriotisms that prevent the three wines being merged into the one *denominazione*, covering red and white.

BIANCO della LEGA A version of Galestro (see below).

BIANCO di NUGOLA A newcomer to the Tuscan scene, made by an enthusiast near Livorno, and worth looking out for in those parts – it is unlikely to be found yet elsewhere. Said to resemble the Verdicchio of the Marche (see chapter 12).

BIANCO VAL d'ARBIA Made of much the same grapes, in much the same way, as the Bianco Vergine Val di Chianti (see above).

FIVIZZANO
FOSDINOVO Two names for very similar wines, mostly red, but some white, from the north of the region, near Massa. Pleasing local wines, to be drunk young.

GALESTRO (10°) A particularly light, dry white wine kept crisp and low in alcohol by picking the Trebbiano early. This is made by Chianti-producers who opted out of the Classico *consorzio* (see p.93). The Bianco della Lega is in effect the same wine made by those who stayed in the *consorzio* (the informal fraternal manifestation of which is the Lega del Chianti). An interesting explanation was given in the September 1981 issue of *Which? Wine Monthly*: Chianti-producers, for the sake of quality, are using less Trebbiano in the percentage of white grapes permitted in the blend (Sangiovese 50 to 80 per cent; Canaiolo, 10 to 30 per cent; Trebbiano Toscano and Malvasia del Chianti, 10 to 30 per cent). These wines use up the surplus and – made by big, efficient firms in modern wineries by modern methods – meet the demand for lighter, fresher Italian whites.

SASSICAIA No *denominazione*, because it is made from a grape – the noble Cabernet Sauvignon – not recognized in Tuscany as D.O.C., though it is in other regions, but one of Italy's finest reds. The grape is that of the greatest clarets, but no claret is wholly Cabernet Sauvignon – all have varying amounts of Merlot and Cabernet Franc; Sassicaia is almost entirely Cabernet Sauvignon, with the smallest possible admixture of the Franc – no Merlot. So, although there is a strong hint of claret about it, there is perhaps an even stronger one of the great California 100 per cent Cabernets, and they are great wines indeed. At a blind tasting of more than thirty Cabernet Sauvignons from a dozen different countries held by *Decanter* magazine in 1978 it was held unanimously to be the best, and I later prophesied in *Punch* that it 'is destined to be as famous as the great Brunello di Montalcino, longest-lived and most expensive of all Italians'.

TIGNANELLO Also ineligible for D.O.C. status because of the inclusion of Cabernet Sauvignon in the blend, though there is much more Sangiovese. Rather harder and more austere than the Sassicaia (above) but a fine wine, worth ageing in bottle.

Chapter 11

Umbria and Lazio

UMBRIA, one of Italy's smallest regions, lies half-way between hip and toe of the long peninsula, between Tuscany and Lazio – Florence and Rome.

Just as we are familiar with the Tuscan landscape – as noted in chapter 10 – from having seen it portrayed in the paintings of the Florentine masters, so the gentleness of the Umbrian countryside, still remarkably unspoiled, is that of Pinturicchio's and Perugino's landscape backgrounds, and a reminder, too, that this is the country of Francis of Assisi, gentlest of saints.

One is even less conscious of vineyards in Umbria than one is in Tuscany where, although production is considerable, the lie of the land keeps sizeable stretches of vineyards secret from the passing motorist. But viticulture is spreading in the region: methods of wine-making have been improved, and the system of *mezzadria*, share-cropping, which lingered on here long after it had been swept away in Tuscany, is now at an end.*

So Orvieto is no longer the only Umbrian wine to be known to the outside world; Umbria now has four other wines with D.O.C. status and, founded by the Lungarotti family, which produces one of them, Torgiano, one of the finest wine museums in Italy.

What links Umbria with Tuscany, apart from contiguity, a great painting tradition, and the similarity of landscape is that Orvieto has almost become a sort of white Chianti.

Officially, there is no such thing as a Chianti *bianco*, but because the great Chianti houses are constantly being asked to supply their

---

* This was the system under which the landlord took half the crop, the other half going to the peasant. The peasant, because he needed wine, oil, wheat, milk and meat, would grow olive trees with vines straggling up their twisted trunks, with ragged wheat or a grazing cow also in the same field. This kind of subsistence agriculture, though picturesque, was not conducive to good wine-growing.

customers with a white wine as well-known and as highly regarded as their red, and are keen to do so, most of them make and market Orvieto, as being geographically the nearest answer, and are members of the Orvieto Classico *consorzio*. Indeed, almost all of them – certainly Antinori and Bigi, Melini and Ricasoli and Ruffino: I think that Frescobaldi is perhaps the only distinguished big Chianti house that does not – have vineyards, or buy grapes, in the district and make their D.O.C. white Orvieto there.

(Note, though, that there is a drive in both the Chianti *putto* and the Chianti Classico *consorzi* to produce Tuscan whites that they hope will eventually be given D.O.C. status (see on pp. 95-6 Galestro and Bianco della Lega).)

Another link with Tuscany is that a good deal of the red wine of Umbria – there is much less red here than white – is made of such Chianti grapes as Sangiovese and Canaiolo, and in the Chianti way.

Compared with Umbria, Lazio is urban, not to say metropolitan, having Rome at its centre, but the Italian countryside comes close to the Italian capital – a mere ten-mile drive from your glass of wine at a café table in the Via Vittorio Veneto or, more humbly, in the Trastevere, and you can visit the vineyard where it was grown, or buy it by the roadside on the old Appian Way, no less, for next to nothing a litre. (Drive another five miles, in the season, and you can attend a meet of foxhounds – established in 1836, the only Italian hunt club in *Bayly's Hunting Directory*, its members as correctly turned out as those of the Quorn or the Pytchley.)

This district, the country of the *castelli Romani*, or Roman castles, in the Alban Hills, south of Rome, is one of Lazio's two main wine-growing areas, the other being around Lake Bolsena, to the north, similar geologically to Umbria's Orvieto country. But the Est! Est!! Est!!! of Montefiascone, the picturesque little town looking out over the lake, is nearer to the *castelli* wines in style than to Orvieto.

All the wines mentioned so far are white, and there are good restaurants in Rome and in the tourist towns of the Alban Hills that serve delicious dishes of fish from the coast between Civitavecchia and Ostia with which to drink them; they also go well with the plump eels of Lake Bolsena. But, as will be seen, reasonably good red wines are grown between hills and sea for those who would rather have red than white to drink with Rome's *abbacchio* and *capretto* – sucking lamb and sucking kid: what the Romans love dies young.

D.O.C. wines of Umbria

COLLI ALTO TIBERINI From the hills of the upper Tiber, north of Perugia. Only recently (June 1980) given D.O.C. status, these white wines (10·5°) are made chiefly from Trebbiano, the red and *rosato* (11·5°) from Sangiovese, like their seniors, Orvieto and Chianti, respectively. I rated them, in an earlier book, as being simple picnic wines; they are now less strong than they were, and more suitable still for drinking under the Italian sun. While being no more pretentious than they were, they are now showing more consistency in style and quality, having reached the dignity of a *denominazione*.

COLLI del TRASIMENO Much the same can be said of these red (11·5°) and white (11°) wines from the shores of Lake Trasimene, scene of Hannibal's resounding victory over Flaminius, from the hills around which comes what many Italian gourmets and great cooks regard as a better olive oil even than that of Lucca. The wines – more red than white, which is unusual in these parts – are not (to my taste) any more distinguished than those of the Colli Altotiberini, though they were awarded their *denominazione* eight years earlier.

MONTEFALCO Again, red and white wines, from the hills south of Assisi, from the same grapes as the wines mentioned above, with the same strength and the same rather run-of-the-mill character; they were given their *denominazione* at the same time as those of the Colli Altotiberini. There is also a red Montefalco Sagrantino or Sagrantino di Montefalco from the grape of the name (12·5°), and a dessert *passito* of the same, strong (14°), sweet and heavily fragrant.

ORVIETO (12°) A great crag of volcanic rock carries the cathedral city of Orvieto, its twenty or thirty thousand inhabitants, and its coach-loads of sightseers six hundred feet above the surrounding plain. This landlocked Gibraltar is honeycombed with caves in which for centuries the wines of Orvieto have fermented and matured.

Also for many centuries, Orvieto was a sweet or

sweetish – *abboccato* – white wine, sold in the characteristic Orvieto wicker-covered, three-quarter litre *pulcianella*, smaller and squatter, but bigger-bellied, than the Chianti *fiasco*, or in the big two-litre *toscanello*. Over recent years, however, the greater demand for a drier wine has been met by the producers, now dominated, as already mentioned, by the Chianti houses, and much more dry wine is produced. As Burton Anderson has put it, new technology has 'transformed Orvieto from a soft, lightly sweet, golden country wine to a crisp, rather dry, pale, straw-coloured cosmopolitan beverage' in a conventional bottle, easier to transport and store, and cheaper to make, than the old *pulcianella*. (Umbrians tell me that recently there has been a very slight, but not very marked, shift back to a rather less dry wine.)

Orvieto, dry or *abboccato*, is made from at least 50 per cent Trebbiano* (sometimes called here Procanico, as in Elba) and is stronger than the taste suggests. The *classico*, like that of Chianti, is produced from a demarcated central zone. It is one of the easiest to drink and most consistent of all Italy's white wines. The *abboccato*, cooled, is far from being heavily luscious, and is delicious with ham and melon or ham and figs.

TORGIANO White (11·5°) and rather more red (12°), all, I think, virtually from one family firm, that of Giorgio Lungarotti, who sells his D.O.C. red under the brand-name Rubesco, his D.O.C. white as Torre di Giano. Both are wines of considerable and – most important – consistent quality that have become highly successful at home and abroad within a mere decade or so (they were not mentioned at all in my book of 1966: I had never heard of them). The red is made from much the same blend of grapes as Chianti (see chapter 10) and is in the same class as the best examples. Aged for three years, it becomes a *riserva*. The white is very like a good dry Orvieto, but modest admixtures of grapes other than Trebbiano make it a little softer and fruitier.

Other wines of Umbria

CANAIOLO Dry red wine made exclusively from one of the minor varieties in the Chianti blend. Not much about.

---

* When Pinturicchio was working on his frescoes in Orvieto cathedral, in about 1500, he had a special clause in his contract stipulating that he should be supplied with as much wine as he wanted of the grapes of Trebbiano.

COLLEPEPE BIANCO A modest wine to be drunk young, made mostly from Malvasia and Sauvignon.

COLLI PERUGINI Sound dry red and white wines, typical of the region, likely soon to be accorded D.O.C. status.

GRECO di TODI Rather full dry white wine, with a heavy scent.

ROSATO di MONTEGABBIONE One of the few *rosato* wines of the region, and a particularly pleasing one, both to nose and taste, made chiefly from the Sangiovese of Chianti.

D.O.C. wines of Lazio

ALEATICO di GRADOLI Richly scented natural (12°) and fortified sweet (17·5°) red wine made from Aleatico grapes grown near Lake Bolsena. Very little made.

APRILIA Mussolini drained the Pontine marshes between the Alban Hills and the sea in 1926, and the same plain became a battlefield after the Allied landings at Anzio in 1944. Since 1980 the town of Aprilia, at its centre, has provided a portmanteau *denominazione* for three wines, Trebbiano, Merlot and Sangiovese, all 'di Aprilia'. Marshland – even reclaimed marshland – is not ideal wine-growing country, and these are decent but pretty commonplace wines, virtually all from the vast Enotria co-operative. Each wine is from at least 95 per cent of its named grape: the Trebbiano (white, 11°) is pleasing, but not in the best Orvieto class; the Sangiovese (11·5°) is *rosato*; and the Merlot (12°), of which there is less than of the others, is a soft, substantial red, easy to drink.

BIANCO CAPENA (11·5°) Not much is made of this white wine from a co-operative north of Rome, from the same blend of grapes as the Colli Albani wines (see below). I have heard the *superiore* spoken well of.

CERVETERI Small amounts are produced in the coastal plain on either side of Civitavecchia of a white (11·5°) and a red (12°), the one from Trebbiano and Malvasia, the other from Sangiovese and Montepulciano. In spite of the *denominazione*, they are still quaffing wines, largely drunk young at local cafés, almost like the new wines of Vienna at *heurige* time.

CESANESE del PIGLIO (10°) **CESANESE di AFFILE or, simply, AFFILE** (12°) **CESANESE di OLEVANO ROMANO** (12°) All from round Frosinone, all red, all from the local grape of the same name, all in dry, sweet, still, *frizzante* and sparkling styles. The Piglio is more plentiful than the other two; the Affile is very hard to find indeed.

COLLI ALBANI (11·5°) **COLLI LANUTINI** (11·5°) Two districts, the Albani the more productive, in the *castelli* country of the Alban Hills, itself officially delimited in 1933, as was the district of Chianti Classico. Co-operatives produce good white wines, dry and *amabile*, from Trebbiano and Malvasia in varying proportions. There is an Albani *superiore* at 12·5°.

EST! EST!! EST!!! (10·5°) Mostly Trebbiano, the rest chiefly Malvasia – roughly the same blend as Orvieto, which it resembles though it rarely, in my opinion, equals, and never surpasses, it. A white wine from the shores of Lake Bolsena, it also resembles Orvieto in having come out of its *pulcianelle* into conventional bottles and having lately moved away from its sweetish style. The story that made its fame and its name is told too often, but it may as well be told correctly.

In the year 1110 Bishop Johann Fugger was on his way from Augsburg to Rome for the coronation of the Emperor Henry V. A devoted amateur of wine, the bishop sent his major-domo, Martin, a day's journey ahead, with orders to write in chalk, on the door of any inn where the wine was good, the word 'Est'. History does not relate how many inns on the long journey were so marked, only that in Montefiascone, the small hilltop town overlooking Lake Bolsena, sixty miles from Rome, the wine was so good that Martin, beside himself with enthusiasm, wrote 'Est! Est!! Est!!!' on the door of the inn.

The bishop travelled no further: his retinue went on to Rome, but he and Martin stayed in Montefiascone, tasting and tippling, until the bishop tasted and tippled himself into his tomb, still to be seen in the church of S. Flaviano, bearing Martin's inscription:

Est. Est. Propter Nimium
Est Hic Jo. Defuk Dominus
Meus Mortuus Est

('On account of too much Est Est Est my master Johannes di Fugger died here' – Defuk being the Italian form of Fugger at the time.)

Not, however, before the bishop had devised in his will that the town of Montefiascone should be his heir on condition that every year, on the anniversary of his death, a barrel of the local wine should be poured over his grave. The custom obtained until the Cardinal Barberigo, Bishop of Montefiascone, ruled that instead of the wine being thus wasted it should go to the local seminary for the young priests where, so far as I know, it is drunk and enjoyed to this day.

It may be that here we have the origin of the old Italian saying, *'Bere come un Tedesco'* – to drink like a German. What I do know more certainly is that some years ago the wife of the then British ambassador to Rome, at a tasting of fine Italian wines, marked a particularly good Barolo on her list with, 'Best! Best!! Best!!!'

FRASCATI (11·5°) A considerable amount is made of this dry white wine. If 12°, it becomes *superiore*. A little *amabile* and *dolce* is made, and a very little *spumante*. It is the best-known of all the *castelli* wines, to some extent because of its quality, but partly, I am sure, because of the town from which it gets its name. A good bottle is a good companion to the Roman *abbachio*.

MARINO (11·5°) Another white wine from the district next-door to Frascati, the wine of which it closely resembles, though there is less of it, and it is perhaps a little fuller in flavour. The *superiore* is 12°.

MONTECOMPATRI COLONNA (11·5°) In 1933 these were two officially distinct districts: the names may still be used separately or together for this dry white wine (12·5° for *superiore*). More Malvasia than Trebbiano in the blend; this may be why it is rather fuller than some of its *castelli* neighbours. Not much available outside its own district.

VELLETRI The *denominazione* covers a fairly plentiful white (11·5°), very like other *castelli* whites, though perhaps a little more rounded, and a red (12°) – the only one in the *castelli* – a fruity wine to be drunk young.

ZAGAROLO The district marches with Montecompatri (see above), from the wines of which its own are indistinguishable.

Other wines of Lazio

ALEATICO di TERRACINA Exactly like Aleatico di Gradoli (see p.102).

ANAGNI Red and white wines from near Frosinone, highly regarded but hard to find.

CASTELLI ROMANI Generic name for the wines of the area that do not qualify for such *denominazioni* as Frascati and the others – not always because of lower standards but sometimes because they are not grown in a recognized, delimited, area. The general level is very high.

CECUBO The name is familiar to readers of Cicero and Horace but, as Felice Cùnsolo has pointed out (and as he could have done of Falerno), the soil may be the same, but are the wines? This is a soft red, with a spiciness to the nose, from the coast near Gaeta.

FALERNO del LAZIO White and red wines from around the Bay of Gaeta, which dispute with a wine of Capua (see under Campania) descent from Horace's Falernian. There is a big, dark red and a dry or a sweetish golden version.

MORLUPO Very like Bianco Capena (see p.102).

NETTUNO A white wine made from much the same grapes as the *castelli* wines, but from near the coast at Anzio, and not in the D.O.C. class.

Chapter 12

Marche, Abruzzo, Molise

MARCHE is the Italian equivalent of the English word 'marches', as in Welsh marches and marcher lords; the area is so-called because it consists of what were frontier provinces of the Frankish empire and the Pope's dominions.

Along with Abruzzo and Molise to the south it still forms a sort of border state between north and south, culturally, economically and gastronomically. This is not so with the two neighbouring regions in the same latitude on the west: Lazio is dominated by Rome and, unlike Abruzzo, was never under Spanish rule; nor was land-locked Umbria, more akin to Tuscany in character and outlook than to its eastern neighbours.

What is officially called Abruzzo is still widely known, and referred to, as the Abruzzi, for there are two clearly defined parts of the region, once formally recognized as such – mountain Abruzzo and maritime Abruzzo. Virtually all the region's wines come from the slopes between the two.

Chiefly, though, this is mountain country; here the Apennines reach their highest points in the Gran Sasso, snow-capped for ten months of the year, and the Maiella. Golden eagles sweep and swoop over the brown bears, the wolves and the chamois in the great national park, and cross-gartered bagpipers come down from the mountains to play for city revellers at Christmas. Here, too, in Abruzzo, were bred such formidable fighters as Rocky Marciano, Rocky Mattioli and the flamboyant patriot, pilot, poet and philanderer, d'Annunzio.

This is mostly simple country where simple peasants cook deliciously simple food, and it is relatively little visited by tourists. The one truly classic wine of these parts, Verdicchio, must be better known by name to foreigners than the region it comes from.

Generally speaking, the wines of the Marche are lighter and more stylish than those of Abruzzo; more are grown there of the classic grapes of the north such as Trebbiano (white) and Sangiovese (red). The region enjoys more of such tourism as there is, and there is probably more of a demand, both from foreign visitors and from visitors from the great cities of northern Italy, for more delicate types of wine.

Abruzzo, though it does not stretch quite so far south as Lazio (L'Aquila, its capital, is farther north from Naples than is Rome), qualifies for investment capital from the Cassa per il Mezzogiorno, the government body for the development of the south, and much has gone into co-operative vineries, *consorzi* of private growers, experimental vineyards, replanting, and the like. As a result, quality and consistency have certainly improved in recent years, but the reds, particularly, of the region are big, hearty wines, like those of the other regions of the south, well suited to the rich local stews of mutton, baby lamb or pork, the brown beans stewed with jellyish, trotter-like strips of baby-pork rind, and the huge white olives, stoned, stuffed and fried.

Molise, though administratively separate, is to be regarded as a small cultural, scenic and gastronomic southern extension of Abruzzo; as yet it has no D.O.C. wines.

D.O.C. wines of Marche

BIANCHELLO del METAURO (11·5°) The Metauro is the river that runs into the Adriatic to the south of the pretty coastal town of Pesaro, Rossini's birthplace (there is a Rossini museum); from its valley comes this dry white wine, made from the Bianchello grape, which goes well with the local fish stews. Rather lighter in alcohol and in the mouth than the much more plentiful and better-known Verdicchio (production is about one-twelth), and to many visitors more appealing in consequence.

BIANCO dei COLLI MACERATESI (11°) A lighter white wine still, partly because it is made largely from the Trebbiano of Tuscany, partly because it is grown in high vineyards in the hills in the south of the region, and thus in a cooler micro-climate. Production, though, is smaller even than that of Bianchello (above), and it is not easily found far from Ancona, where they drink it, of course, with the local fish.

FALERIO dei COLLI ASCOLANI (11·5°) There is even more

Trebbiano (a minimum of 80 per cent of the total blend as against 50) in this white wine than in the Colli Maceratesi (above), and this is also a hillside wine. It is a little stronger, though, and perhaps rather more fruity; there is also more of it about.

ROSSO CONERO (11·5°) Mostly from Montepulciano grapes, like the red wines of Abruzzo (see below), from the slopes of Mount Conero, near Ancona; but, unlike the Abruzzo reds, they are sometimes made in the same way as the Chianti that is made to be drunk young, which gives a greater freshness to the wine when it is so used, when it is fruity to nose and palate.

ROSSO PICENO (11·5°) Far and away the most plentiful of the red wines of Marche; something like five or six times as much is produced as of the Conero (see above); it is very good, too, probably because it is made mostly from the Sangiovese grape of Tuscany, grown on the hills that slope down to the sea near the vineyards that produce Bianchello (see above). Bruno Roncarati recommends it as an accompaniment not only to the stuffed olives already mentioned, which are a local speciality (*all' Ascolano*, after the town of Ascoli-Piceno, which also gives its name to the wine), but also to another local delicacy, wild pigeon roasted on the spit.

SANGIOVESE dei COLLI PESARESI (11·5°) Very similar to the Piceno (above), but from farther north, near Pesaro.

VERDICCHIO dei CASTELLI di JESI (12°) One of the best-known of Italian white wines, abroad and at home, especially on the holiday coast of Emilia-Romagna, to the north. From the Verdicchio grape, grown in the valley of the Esino river, on which the picturesque medieval walled town of Jesi stands, south of Ancona. It would be a mistake to be put off by the desperately fancy-shaped bottles into which it is put, fit only for the bedside lamps of seaside boarding houses: this is a firm, full-flavoured wine, with a refreshingly tart finish, perhaps a bit more positive in character than Italy's other most famous white wine, Soave, and similarly suitable as an accompaniment to the fish stews and fish-fries of the Adriatic coast.

Some is made as is some Rosso Conero, to be drunk young, and is all the fresher for it; some, from the heartland of the delimited D.O.C. district, is entitled also to call itself *classico* – I do not know that it is necessarily better. There is a *spumante* and a *spumante amabile*, neither of them as eminent among Italian sparklers as the still wine is among the still white wines of the country. Still or sparkling, it is a wine to drink young: Bruno Roncarati suggests no more than three years old.

VERDICCHIO di MATELICA (12°) I would be hard put to it to distinguish this Verdicchio from the one above with the so much better-known name. It comes from farther south, not far from the Bianco dei Colli Maceratesi district (see above). There is nothing like so much of it as of the Jesi but, when found, it is probably cheaper and little, if at all, inferior. Also to be drunk young.

VERNACCIA di SERRAPETRONA (11·5°) A sweetish and/or sweet sparkling red wine, limited in production and, I imagine, in appeal, save to those who like the Lambrusco of Emilia-Romagna (see chapter 8) in its sweeter form – which Americans do and I do not.

Other wines of Marche

COLLI MARCHIGIANI The white chiefly from Trebbiano, the red from Sangiovese and Montepulciano. Goodish country wines.

MONTEPULCIANO della VALLE del NEVOLA A sturdier red than the above.

TREBBIANO delle MARCHE A decent white wine from a classic grape, the must sometimes kept longer than usual on the skins, which gives depth, colour and flavour. To be drunk very young before these same qualities develop into coarseness.

D.O.C. wines of Abruzzo

MONTEPULCIANO d'ABRUZZO Here, Montepulciano is the name of the informing grape, which seems to be peculiar to Abruzzo: this red wine is not to be confused with Vin Nobile di Montepulciano of Tuscany, where Montepulciano is a place-name, and where the wine is made from the same Sangiovese as Chianti and Brunello.

Montepulciano is grown widely on the eastward slopes of the

Apennines, and is much more plentiful than the region's one D.O.C. white wine (see below). It is to be found in various strengths, according to the house style of different producers, some individual, some co-operatives: the minimum by law is 12°, but I have come across, and been pretty well bowled over by, powerful bottles at 14°, and it is always rich and full – sometimes too much so. Given two years of age it may be entitled *vecchio*. There is also a deep pink *Cerasuolo* that I believe to be entitled to the *denominazione*, which seems just as big in the mouth as its more deeply coloured cousin.

TREBBIANO d'ABRUZZO This white wine, too, can vary in strength from the legal minimum of 11·5° to as high as 12·5°, but is a different thing altogether from the red Montepulciano (above). It is very much lighter, not merely as a white may generally be supposed to be lighter than a red (often it can be 'bigger') and not only in colour but in *style*: though fruity, it is light as Italian white wines go, whereas the Montepulciano is heavy by the standards of Italian reds. It is a northern wine in character (the Trebbiano is a grape from the north); the Montepulciano is southern. Even so, my advice to foreign visitors is to seek out the Trebbiano of the lowest alcoholic degree.

There is a dry Trebbiano *spumante* made by the *Charmat* or *cuve close* method, sold under the brand-name Bruttium Brut. I am not sure whether it is entitled to the *denominazione* or whether that is reserved only to the still Trebbiano; it is made by one house only, and makes a more than merely acceptable aperitif.

Altogether, there is only about a quarter as much white as red Abruzzo wine, but as there is only about a quarter as much fish as meat on Abruzzo tables there is plenty of wine appropriate to each particular dish. It is interesting that experiments are being made in Abruzzo with the riesling of the Alto-Adige.

Other wines of Abruzzo and Molise

MOLISE BIANCO, ROSSO and ROSATO Cadets of the Montepulciano and Trebbiano families of Abruzzo (see above), and drinkable in country *trattorie* with the hearty local dishes.

MONTUPOLI A white wine made from Montepulciano – the only Italian white wine, I am told, made from black grapes; the French would call this a *blanc de noirs* (like some champagne).

Worth looking out for, especially to drink with some of the rich, hot *antipasto* dishes of the region.

MOSCATO COLLE MORO and MOSCATO TORRE dei PASSERI Sweet muscat dessert wines. There is a Moscato di Molise, too, not yet given official blessing.

TEATINO Red, white and *rosato*.

Chapter 13

Campania, the Basilicata, Calabria

THE story goes that, on the seventh day, the Almighty looked down upon what he had created and, when his eye fell upon the Bay of Naples, he was so moved by its beauty that he shed a tear. From that tear came the first vine, and from that vine Lacryma Christi.

The legend seems to confuse father and son. In any case, at the time of writing, Lacryma Christi, in spite of its being easily the best-known name among the wines of Campania, and however august its legendary origin, is still only under consideration by that lesser body, the *Comitato Nazionale per la Tutela della Denominazione d'Origine*, whereas eight others have already been granted it.

First of all in Campania, and among the first three in the whole of Italy, all in May 1966, status was given to the red and the white of Ischia, the holiday island in the bay. (It has already been pointed out that some growers' associations were quicker than others to apply for recognition, and that some delays are for technical reasons – see chapter 3.) So tribute is duly paid to the luxurious, pretty picture-postcard side – Capri and Ischia, Amalfi and Positano – of a region that knows, too, the poverty of the Neapolitan back streets, the bare slopes of Vesuvius and the Apennines, and the all too recently earth-quake-ravaged countryside.

This is a rewarding region to visit, vibrant with life and southern exuberance. It is the country of *pizza* and *pasta*, and of the Nea-politan music-hall songs of a century ago, 'Santa Lucia' and 'Ciribiri-bin', 'Funiculi, Funicula' and 'Surriento', which visiting Americans, believing them to be traditional throughout Italia, demand to have played by the Piazza San Marco orchestras of Venice, where they are as alien as would be 'Anchors Aweigh' and the Eton Boating Song.

I do not think that the wines of Campania would be similarly mis-understood. There is no wine here so distinguished as to be mistaken for one of the great wines of the north, but many whites that go down well with the octopus and squid, mussels and clams, of Posil-lipo and Santa Lucia, and some fewer reds for the dishes typically rich in tomato and cheese and meat and garlicky sauces.

The Basilicata

Save for a rich coastal strip under the instep of Italy, the Gulf of Taranto, this is a wild region of mountain, moorland and mosquitos, its uplands bitterly cold in winter and sun-scorched in summer, as poor a wine-producing region for quantity as neighbouring Apulia is rich. Its one D.O.C. wine, though, is one of the better reds of Italy's deep south and highly enjoyable with the roasted long, thin pork sausages (*salsiccia lucana*) of the region, kid with artichokes, and *zucchini* baked with yellow peppers, tomatoes and cheese.

Calabria

Some Calabresi – consumers, at any rate – do not take their wines too seriously. In the restaurant at the best hotel in Reggio di Calabria, capital of the region, there is only one red and one white Calabrian wine (both Ciro) in a long wine-list, and at the Conti restaurant, which ought to be in the running for a Michelin star, wines from Tuscany and the Veneto each outnumber the local wines by two to one.

There are few co-operatives here, which may be why viticulture and vinification techniques have lagged behind those of Sicily and Sardinia; local producers will admit frankly that they lag behind the French, especially in producing white wines that will keep their freshness and colour. They do not all agree with each other as to which wines would qualify as being *con indicazione geografica*, and those that would be positively thus classified are less distinguished that many from other regions. I met no one in Calabria who would claim that there are local wines undeservedly overlooked, and none is listed here as such.

Production, though, is considerable, and techniques are

improving, as in every other part of Italy that was once backward – though not always at the same pace. In restaurants that do not keep big stocks and that know how to look after and serve them, young whites go well with the local fish, but the most rewarding wines of Calabria are the full *superiore* and *riserva* reds, to be drunk with the rich meats and highly flavoured *antipasti* of the region.

The future of Calabrian wine is promising, so long as the producers investigate their northern and overseas markets and make especial efforts to produce lighter wines, consistent in style and quality.

D.O.C. wines of Campania

CAPRI One *denominazione* covers the red and the white Capri wines. At one time, wine made from the same grapes and in the same way as those of the island, but on the Sorrentine peninsula, which is geologically identical, were also called Capri; this is not now permitted under the wine law, which gave Capri its *denominazione* in 1977.

The white (11°), from Falanghina and Greco, is full and dry, with a pretty bouquet and a rather bitter after-taste, good with fish or to sit over at a café table.

Only some 10 per cent of Capri wine is red, and it is not so highly thought of as the white. Made from Piedorosso (11·5°), it is lightish in colour and, by southern Italian standards, in body sufficiently so, according to local custom, to be drunk with fish in tomato sauces as well as with meats and *pizze*.

FIANO di AVELLINO (11·5°) Production has always been small – and may well be smaller still since the earthquakes of late 1980 – of this white wine from the grape of the same name, rather fuller in flavour than the Capri white.

GRECO di TUFO (11·5°) The 1980 earthquakes may well have affected production of this wine, too, but there is normally five times as much of it as of Fiano, and it received D.O.C. recognition in 1970 – eight years earlier. Greco, the name of the grape, is a reminder that this was once part – a great part, as the ruined temples of Paestum bear witness – of Magna Graecia, while Tufo, the name of the commune the wine comes from, also means volcanic rock, a reminder of the volcano to which we owe those other ruins, of Pompeii and Herculaneum.

This is a white wine not unlike that of Fiano nearby, but with a more pronounced bouquet and perhaps a stronger back-taste.

ISCHIA Originally three separate *denominazioni*, one now covers red, white and white *superiore*. Only 8 per cent of the island's wine is *bianco* (11°), and 22 per cent is *rosso* (11·5°) (similar to that of Capri, above), while 70 per cent is *bianco superiore* (12°). This differs from the *bianco* in being made from rather less of the Forastera grape and more of the Biancolella; production of grapes per hectare and of wine from grapes is also more limited, and the fermentation process is different.

Naturally, then, the *superiore* is *superiore* – fuller, richer, stronger, recommended in official booklets as good with onion omelettes, lobster and suchlike flavoury foods, whereas the *bianco* is for herb omelettes and simpler shellfish, such as oysters. Often I would prefer the *bianco*, but there is no need to say how much harder it is to get in a restaurant: less of it available, and less profit to be made out of it . . .

LACRYMA CHRISTI See entry following Vesuvio, below.

SOLOPACO (12°) From the same general district as Fiano, Greco di Tufo and Taurasi. The white is finer and more fragrant, to my taste, than Fiano and Greco, no doubt because it is made largely from the more classic grapes, Trebbiano Toscana and Malvasia di Candia.

The *rosso* and *rosato* also benefit by being made to a great extent from the Sangiovese, which in more northerly regions makes good wines such as Chianti. Both red and pink go well with local rabbit and hare dishes – purists, I suppose, would choose the pink with the rabbit, the red with the hare.

TAURASI (12°) Little is produced of this red wine, from much the same area as Solopaco (see above). It is made chiefly from the Aglianico, widely grown in those vineyards of southern Italy that are planted in volcanic soil. Its name is said to derive from *Ellenico*, another reminder that this was once part of Magna Graecia. It makes a good, mouth-filling wine that at its best (and it varies) has reminded me of the Barbera of Piedmont; given a chance, it would perhaps age well in bottle.

115

VESUVIO (11°) Under official consideration, at the time of writing, for D.O.C. status. The red is similar to those of Capri and Ischia (see above), and there is an *amabile* as well as a dry white, the latter being rather sharp.

LACRYMA CHRISTI Out of alphabetical order here because the sparkling and the sweet white Lacryma Christi (12°) are simply the *spumante* and the *liquoroso bianco* versions of Vesuvio (above) and may bear either name – not yet a *denominazione*. There are also a red and a *rosato* (10·5°) similar to, but lighter than, those of Capri and Ischia.

Other wines of Campania

AGLIANICO d'IRPINIA
BARBERA della PROVINCIO di AVELLINO Both red wines – poor relations, so to speak, of Solopaco and Taurasi (above), though the Barbera grape might have been expected to give a more interesting result.

CONCA Red wine of some style, usually drunk young in modern restaurants, though sharp under the youthful fruitiness and rather heady. Good with rich spicy or herby dishes.

FIANO di LAPIO See under Fiano (above), of which it is a local version.

PANNARANO Robust, hard red wine. It vaguely resembles Taurasi (above), coming from roughly the same area, but is inferior to it.

RAVELLO The exquisite Sorrentine beauty spot gives its name to undistinguished but, in so pretty a place, highly acceptable red, white and *rosato* wines. The *rosato* is a little sweeter than the red and the dry white, but there is an *amabile* white that is sweeter still.

SAN GIORGIO del SANNIO A meaty white wine, not unlike the Greco di Tufo (above) from near by, but with a more positive, sharper, finish.

D.O.C. wine of the Basilicata

AGLIANICO del VULTURE (11·5°) From the name of the grape (see under Taurasi, above). Vulture is the extinct volcano on the lower slopes of which it grows, producing a sound, dry, fragrant red wine, less overwhelming than those of neighbouring Apulia, perhaps because of a cooler micro-climate, perhaps because of the volcanic soil. There is also a fuller, deeper, three-year-old *vecchio* (12·5°), and a sparkling version that does not commend itself to me.

Other wine of the Basilicata

MOSCATO del VULTURE (14°) Typically aromatic golden dessert wine. The *spumante* version is not in the same class as those of the north, but pleasant enough, well-chilled.

D.O.C. wines of Calabria

CIRO There is probably more Ciro produced in Calabria than all the other wines of the region put together, and 80 or 90 per cent of it is red. (Official figures do not distinguish between red and *rosato*, but there is little of the latter, and only some 10 per cent of the total is white.)

As can be expected, quality varies, but it is worth looking out for the wine entitled to the name and the neck-label *classico*, from the middle of the delimited district around Ciro itself on the ball, so to speak, of the Italian foot and a *riserva* for preference, which requires three years' ageing. Such a wine can be full, round and satisfying.

The red and the *rosato* are made almost entirely of Gaglioppo grapes; the *rosato* is pleasant enough but undistinguished – both reach a formidable 13·5°. The white (12°) makes a good though substantial aperitif served cold, but there are better Calabrian wines, made from the Greco di Bianco grapes, to go with the tastier fish dishes.

117

DONNICO (12°) More delicate in taste and less powerful than the red Ciro. It is made from only half as much of the Gaglioppo grape, and a variety of others.

GRECO di BIANCO The name is confusing – notice the 'di'. It is in fact a white wine, but it comes from around a small town called Bianco, and is sometimes known as Greco di Gerace. To most tastes it is a dessert wine, but although sweet and with a flowery bouquet it is not cloyingly luscious; the locals drink it as an aperitif with their spicy, peppery *antipasto*. From the Greco grape; the strength is not yet officially laid down, but must be considerable.

LIMENZIO (12°) There is a white, but so far only the red has been granted its *denominazione*. Lightish in colour and body; made from several varieties of grape, among which the Greco Nero and the Nerello Mascalese predominate.

MELISSA The white (11·5°) is a kind of dry Greco di Bianco (see above) and made largely from the same grapes. Not often met with, but would be worth trying in a modest fish restaurant on the coast.

The red resembles the Donnico, though it has almost as much Gaglioppo as the Ciro: 12·5°; but with two years' ageing at 13° it qualifies as *superiore*.

POLLINO (12°) **S. ANNA di ISOLA CAPO RIZZUTO** (12°)
SAVUTO (12°) All red wines, all largely Gaglioppo. Fairly full, hearty wines, not widely known nowadays outside their respective areas of production, south and east of Cosenza, though Savuto used to be exported to the United States in the 1860s, perhaps chiefly for immigrants, before the phylloxera struck. All entitled to the honorific *superiore* at 12·5° and after two years' ageing.

There is a white S. Anna, not yet D.O.C. It has more bite and body than the white Ciro, and I would prefer it with one of the tastier fish dishes.

Other wines of Calabria

BIVONGI (12°) Reds from a wide range of grapes.

CERASUOLO di SCILLA (12°) Strong, sometimes sweetish *rosato*.

118

ESARO Red (12°) and dry white (11·5°).

GIOIA TAURO Red; not widely available.

LACRIMA di CASTROVILLARI Also limited production. Similar to Pollino (see above).

MANTONICO di BIANCO Similar to the Greco di Bianco (see above); very small production.

NICASTRO A less distinguished red Limenzio (see above); very small production.

PALIZZO and PELLARO Both full red wines, from the tip of Italy's toe; used to be sent north for blending, but now seeking identities of their own.

SQUILLACE White wine drunk locally, very young.

VAL di NETO A non-D.O.C. Melissa (see above).

VERBICARO Rather full dry white (12°) and dry red (12·5°), similar to the Melissa white and red (see above).

Chapter 14

Apulia

ONLY a very few years ago, such books – my own among them – as dealt region by region with the wines of Italy lumped Apulia along with Calabria and the Basilicata into one chapter, whereas most other regions each had a chapter to itself. Its 'strong sunshine,' I wrote just before the Italian wine law came into force – and I could have said the same for many years longer – 'in addition to, in some parts, the heavy soil, produces strong, coarse wines, the reds used for blending and the whites as a base for vermouth'. The three regions among them produced few wines known by name outside their immediate localities, and fewer still of much interest.

Since 1968, when the red, white and rosé wines of San Severo were granted D.O.C. status, however, seventeen other Apulian wines have been granted their *denominazioni* (and at the time of writing there are others under consideration) – more than all the D.O.C. wines of Calabria, the Basilicata and Campania put together. This is why Apulia now merits a chapter to itself, while Campania takes its place with the two other southernmost regions in a composite chapter.

It may well be, however, that the Apulian producers have been too eager in applying for, and authority too ready to allow, D.O.C. recognition, for what I wrote in 1965 is still largely true. Some wine-growers are patently disappointed that wines that now have official names and titles of their own are little more regarded in the outside world than when they were sent north for blending or consumed only as carafe wines in countryside *trattorie*.

For the Pugliesi did not, as did the Sicilians and the Sardinians, modify the style of their wines to suit their new status, and most of them are still heavy and unsubtle compared with those of northern Italy and of other European countries. There are reasons for this. In spite of its attractions – from the great Hohenstaufen castle that looks out over Lucera in the north to the baroque beauties of Lecce in the deep south; the long, empty beaches; those strange little prehistoric buildings, the *trulli*, around Albarobello; and the deep, dark forests and craggy cliffs of the Gargano peninsula, the spur on Italy's boot – Apulia is relatively little visited by foreign tourists or holiday-makers from the north to demand in hotels and restaurants good wines of styles to which they are accustomed at home or in more worldly-wise tourist regions.

Sicily is luckier in this respect, and both Sicily and Sardinia are luckier in that more money is made available by their semi-autonomous regional governments for new wineries, experimental vineyards, replanting and the like, than the mainland regions can hope for from the *Istituto per l'Assistanza allo Sviluppo del Mezzogiorno* (I.A.S.M.) – the body set up to develop and enrich the traditionally poverty-stricken south. Whether the deeply conservative peasant wine-growers are forward-thinking enough to take advantage of such aid if it were available is open to doubt; they tend to answer suggestions that they should aim to make their wines lighter, in body and in alcohol, if, as they say, they want them to be more commercially successful abroad and in the north, with the resentful, 'but then they wouldn't be *our* wines'. Yet the University of Bari, where a good deal of oenological research is now going on, is ready and able to give help and advice to those who want it, and keen enough to seek financial support from official sources.

One problem arises from Apulia's having sought and been granted early D.O.C. recognition for some of its wines. Once a *denominazione* has been granted to a wine, it is difficult, if not impossible, to change the variety of grape it is made from, the way the vine is trained and pruned, the production per hectare, the siting of the vineyards, or the alcoholic strength. The growers of Apulian wines could, no doubt, change the style of their wines, as the Sicilians and the Sardinians have done, to suit outside markets, but dare they lose their *denominazioni*?

Meanwhile, as will be seen below, there are some few reasonably light white wines to drink with the excellent fish dishes of the coastal towns and villages – the Pugliesi do admirably tasty things with mussels and swordfish steaks and other fish with olives. The deeply pink *rosato* wines are as full-bodied as the reds themselves for the beef-and-onion and rabbit-and-caper stews. And at vintage time in Carosino, near Taranto, the fountain spouts wine, as in other happy little Italian vineyard villages – an annual reminder that Apulia produces more of the blissful beverage than any other region of Italy, which produces more than any other country.

D.O.C. wines of Apulia

ALEATICO di PUGLIA Sweet red muscat wine, similar to those from the grape of the same name grown in other parts of Italy but, it seems to me, less fragrant than some. There is an unfortified *dolce naturale* (13°) and a fortified *liquoroso* (16°).

AGLIANICO del VULTURE (11·5°) Grown on the border with the Basilicata and exactly like the much better-known wine of that region (see chapter 13). One sometimes comes across an Aglianico Castellanta, presumably the same wine from a more narrowly defined district.

ALEZIO See under Rosato del Salento (below), which at the time of writing (late 1981) is still a *vino da tavola* but is said to be about to be promoted. Alezio is a specifically defined Rosato del Salento.

BRINDISI (12°) Red and *rosato*, from the south of the region, made from the Negroamaro grape and, like the other wines of southern Apulia, not only pretty strong but heavy in the mouth and in the head.

CACC'E MMITTE di LUCERA (11·5°) A red wine from the district around Lucera, in the north of Apulia. The odd and, it would seem to English eyes, virtually unpronounceable name derives from a dialect phrase indicating taking out and putting in. This refers to a local technique, according to which fresh grapes are still being put into the fermenting vat as must is drawn off.

However carefully it is explained, the method remains a mystery to me; I can report only that it results in a red wine rather lighter in colour, character and alcoholic strength than those of the Salentine plain in the peninsula that forms the southern end of Apulia. So much lighter, indeed, that some locals consider it an inadequate accompaniment to dishes (even an official brochure suggests this) 'with pungent and strongly flavoured sauces. May be served cool with salami.' But most northerners would regard it as stout-hearted enough for any meat dish. Serve cool, though, as one might a Beaujolais, especially with a meal out of doors under the hot southern sun.

CASTEL del MONTE Also, like the wine above, from the hillier north of Apulia; also grown in the shade of a great Hohenstaufen castle, like that at Lucera – this one near Andria – hence the name of the wine; also lighter than the wines of the southern plain. The *denominazione* applies to red, white and *rosato* wine, half the total production being *rosato*, 30 per cent red, 20 per cent white. The *rosato* (11·5°) is the most important in quality as well as in quantity; it is unusual among Italian pink wines that share a *denominazione* with a red in that it is not made from the same grape, taken off the skins more quickly. It is made chiefly from the Bombino Nero, with only a little Nero di Troia, which is the chief grape in the red. The Bombino is a particularly good grape for a *rosato* because it ripens into dark and light berries on the same bunch. Nothing like so deep in colour as the pink wines from the south of the region, but more like what foreigners expect a pink wine to be.

The greater lightness is due partly, no doubt, to the variety of grapes but also to the rocky soil and to the relatively (for Apulia) cool micro-climate enjoyed by the vineyards, most of which are between about five hundred and a thousand feet above sea-level. It is also perhaps relevant that here, in the north of the region, more is being done in changing from the low *albarello* vine-growing system, which produces coarse wine because of the heat reflected on to the fruit from the soil, to the taller *espalieri*.

The red Castel del Monte is also lighter in body and alcohol (12°) than most of its counterparts from farther south and good with grills and roasts. With three years' ageing and 12·5° it may be styled *riserva*. A particularly good example is the one produced by the Corato family's Rivera winery, responsible for more than half the production of Castel del Monte wines – this is brand-named Falcone, hawking having been one of the favourite outdoor sports of Eupesov Frederick II. He wrote a learned treatise on the sport and pursued it in the countryside surrounding his great castle here where, according to the English version of the Rivera publicity pamphlet, 'he liked to have around him artists, writers and cultured ladies of staggering beauty'.

The white Castel del Monte is colourless, fairly light (11·5°) and made chiefly of the Pampanuto grape. Not so distinguished among whites as are the red and, especially, the *rosato* of their kind, but crisp and clear and easier to drink than most whites of the south.

It is interesting to note that although a wide range of other grapes is permitted, each wine has to be made from at least 65 per cent of its main variety.

COPERTINO (12°) Red and a small amount of *rosato*, typical of the Salentine wines. See under Leverano (below).

LEVERANO Red, white and *rosato* from around Lecce, typical of this part of Apulia, the Salentine peninsula. The red and *rosato* (12°), from Negroamaro and others, both deep in colour and full-bodied, are quite without finesse; the white (11°), from Malvasia Bianca and others, is similarly unsubtle.

LOCOROTONDO (11°) Lightish, fruity white from the Adriatic coast between Bari and Brindisi; good enough with the local fish. Made from Verdeca and Bianco d'Alessano.

MARTINA or MARTINA FRANCA (11°) White wine named after the commune in which it is made, in the same area as Locorotondo (above) and in effect the same wine. Small production. There is also a sparkling version.

MATINO (11·5°) Red and *rosato* Salentine wines, lighter than some but similar to Leverano (see above).

MOSCATO di TRANI One of the strongest but not one of the finest white muscat wines of Italy. A flavoury dessert wine either in its *naturale* (15°) or fortified *liquoroso* (18°) form.

OSTUNI The *denominazione* applies to a white, Bianco di Ostuni, and a red called, after its grape, Ottavianello di Ostuni, of which little is made. They come from the northern edge of the Salentine plain, east of Brindisi, where the hills begin, and are a little less heavy than the Salentine wines – the white (11°) with a sharp, refreshing finish, the red (11·5°) not much deeper in colour than a darkish *rosato*.

PRIMITIVO di MANDURIA (14°) Little is produced of this wine from around Taranto, the grape of which is so called not because it is 'primitive' but because it is *primaticcio*, early. It is a strange grape, said to be related to the mysterious Zinfandel of California. The first bunches to ripen used to be gathered in August – said to be each year the earliest vintage in Europe – so that the young wine could be sent north in good time to strengthen wines of the same year. Now, an immensely hefty red table wine is made, stronger even than most of its Salentine neighbours and sweetening to an *amabile* level with age. There are *dolce naturale*, *liquoroso dolce* and *liquoroso secco* versions, all very strong.

ROSSO BARLETTA (12°) **ROSSO CANOSA** (12°) **ROSSO di CERIGNOLA** (12°) One would have to be an expert indeed to be able to distinguish between these three hearty Salentine reds – all from Uva di Troia. It is possible that the Cerignola is a little more highly thought of, and ages better: with three years' ageing and at 13° it may call itself *riserva*. There is a particularly dry Cerignola brand-named Torre Quarto that is perhaps a cut above some others. The Canosa may call itself a *riserva* and the Barletta an *invecchiato* after two years, but these are all hair-splitting differences.

SALICA SALENTINO Typical Salentine red (12·5°) and *rosato* (12°) wines named after the commune they came from. See under Leverano (above).

SAN SEVERO Red, white and *rosato* wines made in considerable quantities in the Foggia plain. The white (11°) is made from roughly equal proportions of Bombino Bianco and Trebbiano Toscana, and it may be this latter variety that gives it more suppleness than the heavier whites from the plain to the south. Similarly, the red and the *rosato* (both 11·5°), though made almost wholly from the heavy Montepulciano of Abruzzo, do usually contain some, if only a little, of the more aristocratic Sangiovese of the north, and benefit accordingly. There is said to be a sparkler made from the white, but it has never come my way.

SQUINZANO (12·5°) Red and *rosato* Salentine wines; there is a red *riserva* at 13°. See under Leverano (above).

Other wines of Apulia

CASTELLANA GROTTE Red, white and *rosato* from the Bari area.

GIOIA del COLLE Red wine from Primitivo grapes. See under Primitivo di Manduria (above).

NARDO Heavy red Salentine wine named after its commune. See under Leverano (above).

ROSATO del SALENTO Typical Salentine *rosato*. See under Leverano and see also Alezio (both above). Soon to be upgraded, along perhaps with a red and white. There is a brand named Five Roses that is highly regarded locally, but very powerful for a *rosato* at 13·5°, and a rich dry white Donna Marzia.

RUVO PUGLIESE A red from the Bari area, less hearty than some.

TERRA d'OTRANTO (10·5°) Dry, fruity white – one of the lightest of the region.

Chapter 15

Sicily

NOWHERE in the world of wine has the wind of change blown more strongly during the past couple of decades than through Sicily and Sardinia.

In 1965, in an earlier book of mine on Italian wines, I wrote of the bitterness of Sicilian peasants in the grip of wholesale wine-dealers, of the 'coarse and heavy' Sicilian wines 'used largely for blending' and of 'some few pleasant enough table wines to be found in the island, but they do not get exported even to the mainland, let alone abroad'.

As recently as 1974, Sicily had only two D.O.C. wines, Marsala and Etna, and Philip Dallas, in his *Italian Wines*, could write: 'Sicilian standards are mostly non-existent: farmers still plant what they like, harvest when they like, process the wine just how the fancy takes them, all quite independent of any regulation, technology or local planning'.

Yet now, at the time of writing in 1981, there are nine D.O.C. wines and ten *vini da tavola*, E.E.C. recognized, with others awaiting inclusion in these categories, and the Corvo wines, red and white, although not eligible for either status because their grapes do not come from any one region, are well-known throughout the mainland, the United States and Britain – and well deserve to be. After my latest tour of the island I was able to report in *Punch* early in 1981 that 'many vineyards that once provided the grapes either for Marsala or for the vermouth houses of the north' – and I could have added those that went to 'cut' or 'stretch' better-known wines of the mainland and, indeed, of France and Germany, or to make German brandy – 'are being replanted with the classic varieties for decent table wines. By training the vines high instead of close to the ground, in the traditional Sicilian way (which made for coarseness in the wine because of the heat reflected by soil and stones), lighter wines are being made. The creation of vineyards higher on the hillsides than before is producing similar results because of the advantage of a cooler micro-climate. All this is being helped and encouraged by the regional government.' (Sicily has enjoyed a certain measure of autonomy since 1945, with a regional parliament at Palermo.)

The efforts of the Palermo government have been augmented by those of the Regional Institute of Vines and Wines, by financial aid from the central government, by the efforts of the Italian Institute of Foreign Trade, and by the setting up, with official help and encouragement, of co-operatives equipped with every modern device, and research laboratories, experimental vineyards and oenological institutes.

The result is not only that, as I recorded in 1981, I 'enjoyed good table wines from one end of the island to the other – Etna reds and whites in Taormina; a dry white Torre Marina in Marsala, made by one of the old-established Marsala houses, and in Palermo an excellent, fruity but crisp white Rapitala (D.O.C. Alcamo)', but that more and more British and American shippers are importing Sicilian wines. Many of these, if not perhaps all, bear on their labels not only an indication of whether they are entitled by the Italian wine law to proclaim themselves of D.O.C. status but also the formal letter 'Q' – the symbol permitted by the Sicilian authorities to Sicilian products (food as well as wine) that satisfy strict official quality specifications and submit to constant supervision.

Once upon a time, and not all that long ago, the notion would have seemed absurd. Today, the authorities have the requisite knowledge and are admirably strict, and a surprisingly high proportion of Sicilian wines are worthy of the accolade.

D.O.C. wines of Sicily

ALCAMO (11·5°) Virtually colourless dry wine made from Catarratto Bianco (*comune* and/or *lucido*) with no more than 20 per cent in all of Damaschino, Grecanico and/or Trebbiano Toscano, around the town of Alcamo, between Palermo and Trapani, inland from the Gulf of Castellamare. Used to be neutrally bland, largely a basis for vermouth, but quality is improving; at best, it is light and slightly fruity, good with fish (perhaps because of a delicate aniseed flavour that some experts find in it). Good examples come from the family-owned Rapitala vineyard, from the Medoro co-operative, and from a group of growers around Segesta. (There is a local non-D.O.C. wine of much the same sort, named simply Segesta.)

CERASUOLO di VITTORIA (12·5°) A cherry-red wine – hence its name – from the deep south of the island, stronger and fuller-bodied than the colour would suggest, with a herby, flowery scent; good with game. Can be drunk young and fresh, but ages well. Made from not less than 40 per cent Frappato and not more than 60 per cent Calabrese, with up to 10 per cent other varieties permitted; the grapes are fermented quickly and taken quickly off the skins to ensure the characteristic deep pink colour.

ETNA The *denominazione* applies to red, white and rosé wines from the slopes of the volcano. This was the first zone in Sicily to be delimited for D.O.C. (in 1968), but its wines are not the island's most distinguished. The whites are the more plentiful – dry and pleasing to the nose. There is a *bianco superiore* from one particular commune, Milo, made from at least 80 per cent Carricante grapes and with a minimum strength of 12°, rather deeper in colour, flavour and bouquet than the ordinary *bianco* (11°), which has 60 per cent Carricante, up to 40 per cent Catarratto, *comune* or *lucido*, and up to 15 per cent others.

The red is astringent and light-bodied though strong (12·5°), which is no doubt why it ages well; the *rosato* (12·5°) should be drunk young and cool – a good example bears the brand-name Gattopardo. Red and rosé are both made from the same grapes: largely Nerello Mascalese, up to 20 per cent Nerello Mantelato and up to 10 per cent white varieties.

FARO (12°) It took nine years longer for Faro than for Etna to be granted D.O.C status, though it is made near by, from the same grapes and in much the same proportions, and is, to my taste, the better wine – perhaps because of the inclusion of Sangiovese, the informing grape of Chianti, in the other varieties permitted to be added in small proportions to the Nerello strains. It may be that producers delayed their D.O.C. application until production was adequate; it is still small. The wine is named after the lighthouse (*faro*) at the north-eastern tip of the island, and matures after about five years to show more elegance and depth than the red Etna.

MALVASIA delle LIPARI (11·5°) A golden dessert wine from the Aeolian (otherwise Lipari) islands, the best being from the island of Salina. Made from 95 per cent of the grape of the same name into a light, sweet table wine or, by partly drying the grapes into a richer *passito* dessert wine (18°), or, by subsequent fortification and further ageing, into a heavier *liquoroso* (20°). Not to everyone's taste but one of the best of its kind in Italy, to drink with the richly sweet confections – *cassate* – of Sicily or for its own sweet sake after dinner.

MARSALA In 1770, a Mr Woodhouse of Liverpool, visiting Sicily on business, realized that the wines grown under the hot sun and in the dry, iron-bearing soil of the western end of the island closely resembled those from which port, sherry and madeira were made. With his sons, he set up the Marsala firm of Woodhouse, soon to be joined in rivalry with such other English families as Inghams and Whitakers, producing a rich aperitif or dessert wine that in Regency and Victorian times rivalled Madeira.

The English firms survive now only as names owned by the Florio firm, itself part of the great Cinzano group, as well as one of a twelve-member consortium dedicated to moving Marsala into modern times.

The fancy mixtures – with egg, almond or fruit flavourings – do not enjoy D.O.C. status and are being phased out, and Italians are being encouraged to drink the Marsala *superiore*, sweet or dry, as a *vino di meditazione*, which I take to mean a wine for drinking in front of the television set. Meanwhile, as consumption has declined, at home and abroad, many vineyards once providing grapes for Marsala are being replanted with the classic varieties for good table wine – one of the old Marsala houses now produces a sound dry white, Torre Marina.

Basically, the fragrant dry wine made from Catarratto and/or Grillo grapes, with up to 15 per cent Inzolia, becomes Marsala with the addition of grape brandy, a sweet wine made from the same varieties of grape, semi-dried, and young unfermented grape-juice that has been slowly heated until it has become sweet and caramelly. Thus, the wine is fortified, like sherry and port, and partly 'cooked' – to some extent like madeira.

The three D.O.C. grades are:

Marsala *fine* or I.P. ('Italia Particolare') can be dry or sweet; must have four months' ageing and reach 17°.
Marsala *superiore* – L.P. ('London Particular') and S.O.M. ('superior old Marsala') are dry; G.D. ('Garibaldi Dolce') is sweet. Needs two years' ageing, and must reach 18°.

Marsala *vergine* is dry – no concentrated or cooked must is added; it must have five years' ageing and 18°.

Those days are gone when Sandhurst cadets were allowed to drink Queen Victoria's health in Marsala at twopence a glass (an odd break in the tradition of toasting our Hanoverian monarchs in that traditionally Whiggish drink, port), but I am sure that Italian doctors still recommend as a restorative, and Italian wives still make for their husbands as a honeymoon dish – same thing, I suppose – that most delicious of puddings, *zabaglione*: two egg yolks, two teaspoons of sugar, and a sherry glass of dry Marsala for each person, stirred over a slow fire until the mixture thickens, and served immediately.

MOSCATO Of the many sweet wines of Sicily, two in the south-east corner, from Siracusa and Noto, have D.O.C. status, as has that of the tiny island of Pantelleria, half-way to Africa.

Moscato di Noto and Moscato di Siracusa are both made of the Moscato grape (also known as Moscato Giallo or Moscatella). Moscato di Noto *bianco* or *naturale* is a sweet table wine, golden yellow and fragrant (11·5°); the Moscato di Noto *liquoroso* is made of selected grapes and fortified and is thus stronger (22°) and more luscious. There is a D.O.C. entitlement for a *spumante*, but I have not met any.

Production of the Moscato di Siracusa is very small, and there is no *liquoroso* or *spumante* version: it is made from partly-dried grapes (16·5°).

The Moscato di Pantelleria *naturale* is a naturally sweet table wine from a Moscato variety known locally as Zibibbo, or Moscatellone; so is the Moscato Passito di Pantelleria or Passito di Pantelleria, except that it is made from dried grapes and fortified, and so is stronger (23·9° as against 12·5°) and richer. The sweet sparkling version of the *naturale* is also D.O.C. and is sold under the brand-name Solimano.

Other wines of Sicily

CERDESE BIANCO A dry white which owes its crispness partly to its being grown a thousand feet above sea-level in the north of the island, and partly to the small admixture of the Tuscan Trebbiano with the predominating Inzolia (60 per cent) and Catarratto (25 per cent). Especially good with fried fish.

CERDESE ROSSO Full red wine from the same region.

FRAPPATO del VITTORIESE Red wine from Vittoria, the small Spanish-baroque town near Ragusa, in the south. Can be regarded as a young cousin of Cerasuolo (see above) but is made solely from the grape it is named after, with no admixture of other varieties.

GRECANICO di MAZARA del VALLO Pale white wine, slightly bitter, exclusively from the Grecanico grape. Grown in the west of the island, it is reputed to be full-flavoured enough for meat dishes, and also much used not only with fish but also for cooking fish dishes.

NERELLO SICILIANO Red wine, also from the western end of the island, also named after the grape from which it is exclusively made. Not unlike the red Etna.

PIGNATELLO di SICILIA Red wine from a grape that has different names in different parts of the island – Perricone, Nerello di S. Antonio and others. Its quality varies, too, but it is said to be found at its best in the Marsala-Trapani district, where it should serve as a safe choice in small restaurants.

REGALEALI BIANCO 'Almost Alsatian in style' was how I described this dry, fruity white in *Punch* early in 1981. It owes its style partly, perhaps, to its being grown fifteen hundred feet up in the mountains between Enna and Palermo, partly to a modest amount of the elegant French Sauvignon grape added to the basic Catarratto and Inzolia. Certainly one of Sicily's best whites.

ROSSO di SCIACCA A red from the country behind the white-painted, African-looking, seaside town of Sciacca, west of Agrigento. A traditional local wine, now being particularly well made in such co-operatives as Enocarboj, which uses the brand-name Carboj, and Settisoli. Wines bearing these labels (whites and rosés as well as reds, and wines named after their grape varieties) are to be relied on in little shops and *trattorie*, so long as they have been well kept.

VERDELLO SICILIANO A traditional white wine, grown largely by peasants in the old days and all over the west of the island. Now coming up in the world, it is not yet to my mind more than a pleasant picnic wine.

ZIBIBBO dell'isola di PANTELLERIA Dry relative of the sweet Moscato of Pantelleria (see above). To my own taste, it resembles a dry Sauternes, and gives the impression that it would be a sweet wine if it could – there is an underlying earthiness.

As well as the D.O.C. and the recognized *vini da tavola* wines of the island, the Paronetto *Guida ai Vini d'Italia* and Burton Anderson's *Vino* list, respectively, eleven and no fewer than thirty-nine 'other' wines. A pamphlet issued in 1979 by the island's *Assessorato Regionale alla Cooperazione e al Commercio* and the *Istituto Regionale della Vite e del Vino* added eighty-six 'others' to the D.O.C. wines.

Some are wines already listed here, but in their lists bearing brand-names; some have generic names (e.g. 'Rosso di Sicilia') which can mean anything; some have varietal names ('Sangiovese Siciliana'); some are difficult, if not impossible, to find even in their own district. Some, though, deserve recognition, and may have already applied for it – perhaps even been granted it by the time these words reach print; some do not want it, or fail to qualify for some purely technical reason.

Such 'other' wines as I consider should not be overlooked include:

ADRANO Red wine from the slopes of Etna, where some wines may be worthy of the 'Etna' D.O.C. but have failed to qualify.

ALA An acronym from the initials of Antico Liquor (Vino) Amarascato, more of a liqueur, but always listed in the reference books as a wine, whereas the recognized liqueurs, such as Strega, are not. Sweet, semi-dried grapes are fermented in cherry-wood casks to produce a richly scented, strong, sweet wine. Made by Corvo (see below).

AMBRATO di COMISO Heavy white wine made from the same black grapes that produce the Cerasuolo of the district (see above).

CARBOJ See under Rosso di Sciacca, above.

CORVO The most widely sold wine of the island and the best-known at home and abroad, yet not entitled to D.O.C. or even minor status because the grapes used are bought from all over Sicily, whereas all officially designated wines, according to the Italian wine law, must come from a specified area.

Corvo is no longer the property of the ducal home of Salaparuta, though it bears the name and arms. All these were sold, a generation ago, to a private company in which a good deal of regional government money is invested.

Like a champagne or cognac house, Corvo has contracts with growers, and it collaborates with the University of Palermo in advising them, and in running its own quality control and experiments; it is a most impressive organization, making sound, reliable wines. As well as the red and the white, both well up to D.O.C. standard, there are a lighter and more delicate white, Corvo Colomba Platino, in a Moselle-shape bottle; Ala (above); a dry and a sweet sparkling wine, made by the *cuve close* method; and the Stravecchio di Sicilia, not unlike a dry sherry, and served as such.

DAMASCHINO A particularly light white wine from the western end of the island, low in alcohol by Sicilian standards.

DRACENO del BELICE The Saturnia co-operative, in the west of the island, produces a rather full-flavoured *rosato*, a particularly full, dry white and a heavy, heady, powerful red, unusually deep in colour, calling to mind such wines as the 'black' wine of Cahors and the Hungarian Bull's Blood.

ELORO Rather coarse, rather strong red, white and rosé wines from the south-east corner.

FEUDO dei FIORI See under Settisoli (below).

FONTANAMURATA Full, dry, deep-coloured white and, by contrast, a rather light, dry red, both made from Catarratto and Inzolia grapes. They sometimes go under the name of Pachino, from the town that is its commercial centre, sometimes Valledolmo.

MAMERTINO Known to the Romans of Julius Caesar's time, now not easy to find even in Messina or Milazzo, near which cities it is grown. 'The colour of old gold with a pronounced aroma of raisins,' writes Burton Anderson, 'it is best as a lightly *amabile*, soft, smooth dessert wine. A drier version makes a good *aperitivo.*'

PARTINICO Wines of the Marsala and Moscato type, from near

Palermo; the sweet Lo Zucco Moscato and the dry version are good examples.

REGALEALI ROSSO The red has not been given the status accorded to the white (see above) but is similarly distinguished: Edmund Penning-Rowsell of the *Financial Times* has found 'a whiff of claret about it'.

ROCCHE di RAO Delicately fragrant dry white wine, highly regarded locally, though possibly not a good traveller.

SETTISOLI (It may be found under its brand-name, Feudo dei Fiori.) See under Rosso di Sciacca for the red wine. The white is softer and fruitier than many others of the island.

VAL di LURO Among the few wines from the mountainous middle of the island, near Enna, these red, white and rosé wines are among the island's most elegant cheaper wines, perhaps because such classic mainland grapes as Trebbiano and Pinot Grigio (white) and Sangiovese (red and *rosato*) are included in the blend.

LO ZUCCO See under Partinico (above).

Chapter 16

Sardinia

EVERY region of Italy differs from every other region – it is one of the charms of the most charming of European nation-states that this should be so – but none differs more sharply from all the rest than does Sardinia. The island is far more remote from the mainland than is Sicily; the landscape, as D.H. Lawrence observed in his *Sea and Sardinia* (1921), 'very different from Italian landscapes . . . ridges of moor-like hills running away, perhaps to a bunch of dramatic peaks . . . a sense of space, which is so lacking in Italy'. The people, too, in the words of the official guide book, are 'rough and austere', but with 'a keen sense of honour and hospitality'.

A keen sense of humour, too – for it is with a straight face but, I am sure, with ironic pride, that a Sard will tell you that in his much-loved island the sheep outnumber the people by more than two to one – something like three and a half million to one and a half. (Nor, I gather, does the three and a half million include the mouflons – the wild sheep of the mountains, extant only here and in Corsica, and a protected species. There are wild boar here, too, and, to add to the strange feel of everything about Sardinia, flamingoes. The wild boar are good to eat; I am not so sure about the flamingoes . . .)

In area, the island is nine-tenths the size of Sicily, but it is inhabited by fewer than one-third as many people, and produces only one-quarter the amount of wine. Yet empty and largely untamed though it is – except for the Costa Smeralda playground for plutocrats in the north-eastern corner – Sardinia has done even better than Sicily in raising the standard of its wines. It produces twice as many with D.O.C. status, representing 13 per cent in volume of the island's total production, whereas Sicily's proportion of D.O.C. wines is a mere 4 per cent of the total.

Some 80 per cent of all Sardinia's wine comes from the island's forty co-operatives. Over the past twenty years or so, much of the money that both the central government in Rome and the regional government in Cagliari have made available to Sardinian agriculture has wisely been spent on new vineries with modern equipment, experimental vineyards, research and replanting vineyards of coarse, prolific varieties with 'classic' vines from the mainland. It would have been unheard of even a mere decade ago for a Sardinian co-operative to be supplying – as one such is doing at the time of writing – both Harrods and the Waitrose chain of supermarkets. This is a measure of the quality now reached by Sardinian wines, the quantity regularly available and, above all, the consistency of their style and standard.

On a lower level, there is still plenty of cheaper, less distinguished Sardinian white wine available for export in bulk to Germany, where it is bottled with labels bearing German-sounding names in Gothic lettering, surrounded by Rhine maidens and the like – all of which is perfectly legal so long as the E.E.C. regulations are complied with. This means that there must be a legend on the bottle (it is always in small type) indicating that the contents come from another E.E.C. country, or more than one such, and that there must be no stated claim that the wine is German. (No doubt the Germans sweeten the wine somewhat, or arrange for it to be sweetened, either by adding sugar or, much more likely, by adding Süssreserve – unfermented grape-juice.)

This can do no harm to the reputation of Sardinian wines, for if quality is low it will reflect only on the German shippers: there is no mention of any *particular* E.E.C. country on the labels. And such is the Sardinians' pride in their wines, very apparent when I toured the island at the end of 1980, that I cannot believe that they will sacrifice quality for quantity and cheapness, to earn quick and easy money on the German market at the expense of the D.O.C. and other recognized wines that are now beginning to earn a deserved reputation in Britain and the United States.

Meanwhile, the regional authorities have devised a scheme similar to that of Sicily by which products – again food as well as wine – that reach and maintain a specified standard of quality are entitled to bear the symbol 'S'. It is intended, however, that the symbol for wine should be changed, to distinguish it from other products. I cannot think why, and I hope that the change will not lead to utter confusion. In any case, the best indication of quality is what is in the bottle.

D.O.C. wines of Sardinia

CAMPIDANO di TERRALBA (or TERRALBA) (11·5°) Red wine from the richly fertile plain of Campidano, south of Oristano, on the west coast, named after its chief commune. So light in colour as often to be more like a deep *rosato* than a true red; like a *rosato*, it should be drunk young and cool. Chiefly from the Bovale grape, full in flavour and pretty full in strength for its colour.

CANNONAU di SARDEGNA (13·5°) The best-known of the island's table wines, partly because it is widely available, partly because there are many kinds, partly because, this being so, it is of all-round usefulness. Made from the Cannonau grape, peculiar to the island, and grown widely, it can be found *rosato*, as strong and as full as the red, excellent with sucking pig and roast baby lamb, both island specialities. The dry red (*secco normale*) goes well with grills and roasts of darker meat; the *superiore naturalmente secco* (15°) and the *normale* that has had three years or more in wood, thus becoming a *riserva*, with rich stews, as of the island's wild boar.

There are sweet (*dolce*) and semi-sweet (*amabile*) versions of the Cannonau *superiore* that may well appeal less to British and French visitors than to the locals, and there are dry and sweet fortified versions too – *vini liquorosi*, made by adding spirit, as in the making of sherry and port – that seem to me to have an even more limited appeal.

CARIGNANO del SULCIS (11·5°) 'A robust *rosso* and a tasty *rosato*' is how Burton Anderson describes the two versions of this newly designated D.O.C. wine, and I cannot better the description. The red, indeed, and especially the *invecchiato*, with greater age in wood, is remarkably rich and deep for its strength, appetizingly bitter to smell and taste, and an appropriate accompaniment to such local delights as wild boar (in season 'for twelve Sundays', they tell you on the island – December to February, inclusive) and *formaggio arrosto*, which is sheep's milk cheese smokily roasted over an open fire. The *rosato* is lighter to the eye, but as with other

Sardinian wines pretty well as strong and flavoury as the red from the same grape. Both are made almost entirely from the Carignano, and grown mostly in and around the Antioco peninsula, at the island's south-east corner.

GIRO di CAGLIARI (14·5°) Named after its grape, a lightish red to a sort of topaz in colour. There is a dry and a sweet version, and a *liquoroso* of each (17·5°). Suitable as an aperitif or a dessert wine, according to taste.

MALVASIA di BOSA; MALVASIA di CAGLIARI Two D.O.C. entitlements for what are virtually identical golden wines from the Malvasia grape – experts claim to detect a greater character in the Bosa. Similar in style to the Giro (above). Sardinians drink the dry as a table wine with fish, which I would not, though I have found it acceptable enough as a sort of dry, fruity, non-fortified pre-prandial sherry. The dry Bosa is 14·5°, the sweet 15°; the Cagliari dry and sweet are both 14°; all the *liquorosi* are 17·5°.

MANDROLISAI (11·5°) One of Sardinia's soundest and most reliable wines, made from Bovale Sardo, Cannonau and Monica grapes in the middle of the island and named after the hilly region inland from Oristano. A solid, full-bodied red and a *rosato* with the typical backbone of southern Italian pinks. An official local brochure recommends the latter with fish, but I disagree: it is as much a wine for meat dishes as is the red.

MONICA di CAGLIARI (14°) **MONICA di SARDEGNA** (12°) Both from the same grape, Monica, but two rather confusing *denominazioni*: the Sardegna is simply a dry red table wine good with meat and cheese, but there are *dolce naturale* and dry and sweet *liquorosi* (17·5°) versions of the Cagliari, as well as a dry red that is bigger in style and more potent than the Sardegna.

MOSCATO di CAGLIARI; MOSCATO di SARDEGNA; MOSCATO di SORSO-SENNORI (or simply SORSO or SENNORI) All naturally sweet, dessert muscat wines, ranging from 11·5° to 15°, the Sardegna being the lightest; only the Cagliari has a sweet *liquoroso* version (17·5°) as well.

NASCO di CAGLIARI (14·5°) Yet another of the Sardinian D.O.C. wines to be found in natural sweet and dry and *liquoroso* sweet and dry (17·5°) versions. The Nasco grape is neither so luscious nor so heavily aromatic as the Moscato but, as I wrote many years ago of its wine, it has 'a quite charming orange-blossom bouquet, and the faintly bitter under-taste to the sweetness makes it perhaps the most interesting of its type'. But I would still not recommend it, as the official handbook does, to go with shellfish. It is a sipping wine for long summer evenings.

NURAGUS di CAGLIARI (12°) Unlike the above, this really is a wine for fish, pale and crisp, made from the Nuragus grape (there is an etymological connection with the *nuraghi*, the strange, prehistoric, conical stone houses that dot the Sardinian countryside). The simplest version, without *denominazione*, is the typical carafe wine of Sardinia; among the best that have D.O.C. status are those from the Marmilla, Mogoro and Dolanova co-operatives – the brand-name of this last being Parteolla.

VERMENTINO di GALLURA (12°) Amber-coloured dry wine, with a lightly astringent finish, made in the north-east of the island from a mainland grape. Makes a good unfortified, sherry-type aperitif, like Vernaccia (below), though the locals drink the ordinary strength with fish; there is also a *superiore* (14°). There are Vermentinos della provincia di Sassari, del Giudicato, della Romangia and di Monte Santo that do not have D.O.C. rank, but seem of much the same quality.

VERNACCIA di ORISTANO (15°) From the grape of the same name, the island's best-known wine, as is Marsala that of Sicily. Also like Marsala, it is not necessarily its best-loved or most widely drunk – a particularly dry, hard wine with a flavour of bitter almonds. 'Dry and masculine', says Philip Dallas, ' . . . not a wine to play with: only those with good heads can drink it as a table wine, more usually it is used as an aperitif'. That is how most foreigners would take it, but the Sardinians drink it after as well as before meals. There is a similar, but non-D.O.C., Vernaccia di Villasor.

Other wines of Sardinia

GREGU NIEDDU OR GRECU DELL' ORISTANENSE (14°) Gregu Nieddu is the harsh Sardinian dialect version of Greco Nero. This hearty red wine is made of the grape so widely grown on the mainland, in Calabria. Here, production is mostly, or entirely, limited to the Campidano co-operative at Terralba – a gutsy wine to go with gutsy grub.

IERZU The name of a good co-operative that produces red, white and *rosato* wines all, in different proportions, from the Cannonau grape (so that the white is largely a *blanc de noirs*) all well-made, soft, full in flavour, and heavy in alcohol.

A similar co-operative at Dorgali, on the east coast, near the caves that are the homes of the Mediterranean's last seals, makes very similar wines, worth looking for under the Dorgali label, though they do not enjoy D.O.C. or *vino di tavola* status.

PASSITO di ALGHERI Luscious golden dessert wine, made from dried or semi-dried Torbato grapes (see Torbato, below).

SANGIOVESE SARDO For fifty years now, some slow progress has been made in various parts of the island with this Tuscan grape, the great grape of Chianti, the Sardinian version of which I reported on almost twenty years ago as 'a sound red table wine, with more than just a hint of the Chianti fragrance and flavour, but rather stronger and fuller, as one would expect from a sunnier, hotter climate'.

SANT' ANTIOCO In effect, a Carignano del Sulcis (see above) but specifically from the island of Sant' Antioco, off the south-west corner of the island. The more general name applies as well to the adjacent mainland vineyards.

TORBATO A dry white wine from the grape of the same name – 'fresh, clean and tautly fruity', Burton Anderson says of it. This is the result of techniques recently introduced by the enterprising house of Sella and Mosca, founded at the turn of the century by Piedmontese partners, and now campaigning vigorously to produce wines that suit today's taste for wines much lighter than the Sardinian whites of the recent past. Probably the best of the island's whites.

Appendix 1

Vermouth, Sparkling Wines, Vin Santo and Vin Cotto

IN France, there is an *appellation d'origine contrôlée* for the delicately dry, white *vermouth de Chambéry*, but there is no such *denominazione* for vermouth in Italy. It is a manufactured, blended aperitif, and no Italian vermouth will ever be sold on the reputation of a particular variety of noble grape or, like Chambéry, on the name and fame of its birthplace.

Nevertheless, it is based on wine, it is one of wine-growing Italy's best-known and, economically, most important products, and of the two great vermouth-producing countries, Italy produces more than France. There must be at least some modest mention of it in any book on Italian wines.

Aromatized wines were known in classical times, but vermouth more or less as we know it today was first made in Turin in the eighteenth century, the Moscato of the region proving an admirable base with which to blend extracts from the aromatic plants of the nearby Alpine foothills. Tony Lord, in his *World Guide to Spirits* (1979), states that about fifty herbs and other flavourings go into a vermouth and names a couple of dozen; it is significant that the French centres of production, Marseilles and Chambéry, also have multitudinous mountain herbs within reach.

Vermouth production is big business, and Piedmont is still its native region, with Martini e Rossi, Cinzano, Carpano, and Cora in Turin, and Gancia, Riccadonna, and Contratto in Canelli, fifty miles away. Although there is no D.O.C. control, Italian law requires that 70 per cent of anything calling itself 'vermouth' must be pure, natural wine. As Piedmont cannot possibly produce enough nowadays to satisfy the appetite of these vast organizations;

most, if not all, the wine required comes from Sicily and southern Italy. This is sweetened, fortified, flavoured and (for the darker sweet white and the red vermouths) coloured.

The requirement that wine must be the base is, of course, for vermouth only: there are other aperitifs under other names, made of neutral alcohol, sugar and flavourings, which contain no wine at all – Campari is an example. And true wine can be quinined into bitterness, as is Barolo Chinata (see chapter 4), without assuming the name of vermouth.

The various brands of vermouth differ, but the main styles are *bianco* and *rosso*, both sweet, and another, drier white, more after what we used to think of as the French style, labelled *secco* or *bianco secco*, but more usually called for, even by Italians, as 'dry'.

The great vermouth houses, such as those I have named, have the resources and facilities not only for making Asti Spumante (see chapter 4) but for dry white sparkling wines made, unlike almost all Asti – Contratto is an exception – by the champagne method.

Contrary to what most foreigners believe – that Italians like only sweet sparklers – such wines are immensely popular in Italy (which is, after all, France's biggest foreign market for true champagne). Although dearer than Asti, they are cheaper than French champagne, although patently well-bred and well-made from the French varieties of grape in the French way. Typical examples are produced under brand-names by Cinzano, Gancia, Martini and Contratto, already mentioned as vermouth houses, and by Fontanafredda at Alba, also in Piedmont. Perhaps the most distinguished Italian dry *spumante*, though, is that produced by the Ferrari firm (no connection with motor-cars) at Trento – the Ferrari Gran Spumante Riserva is served at presidential banquets and the like. Burton Anderson speaks highly of another *méthode champenoise* sparkling wine from the Trentino, made by Equipe 5, an association of five independent producers, but it has not come my way.

It will have been noticed in previous chapters that the *denominazione* of many D.O.C. dry white wines may be extended to a *spumante*, but this does not necessarily mean that any such *spumante* is made. All of any importance come from the north, mostly from Piedmont. This is not so with *vin santo*, the sweet, rich dessert wine made throughout the country from the white grapes of the district. These are (I generalize) dried on straw after the vintage and not pressed until as late as the following Easter – hence the name, *vin* or *vino santo*, made in Holy Week. Italy's *vini santi*, from the Alps to Etna, vary enormously, but those who like this kind of thing speak especially highly of the *vini santi* of the Trentino and of Ricasoli; of (an oddity) a dry *vin santo* of Montalcino (both the house of Ricasoli and the town of Montalcino are in Tuscany), and of those of Umbria.

Many of the *vini santi* are from northern or central Italy – although, as I have said, much is also made in the south. More specifically southern, perhaps, is *vin cotto* – 'cooked wine' – which I have met in regions as far apart as the Marche and Sardinia, and Burton Anderson has found in Abruzzo. It is made by reducing grape-juice over the fire to less than half its original volume and then bringing it back to its original volume by adding uncooked, unfermented must. After fermentation, it is aged for at least two years; it then produces a sweet, rich (to my mind, sickly) Malaga-like wine of considerable strength.

Appendix 2

Consorzi di Tutela

Piedmont
Consorzio del Gattinara
Vignaioli Piemontesi – Consorzio tra Cantine Cooperative
Consorzio per la difesa del vino tipico di Carema
Consorzio per la tutela dei vini a Denominazione di Origine Controllata
Consorzio per la difesa dei vini tipici di pregio Barolo e Barbaresco
Consorzio per la difesa dei vini tipici Barbera d'Asti e Freisa d'Asti
Consorzio per la difesa dei vini di Caluso
Consorzio Asti Spumante

Lombardy
Associazione Consorzi Vini Lombardi a D.O.C.
Consorzio Vini D.O.C. Oltrepò Pavese
Consorzio difesa Vini Tipici Bresciani

The Veneto
Associazione Vini Veronesi D.O.C.
Consorzio Volontario per la tutela della Denominazione di Origine Controllata dei Vini Colli Euganei
Consorzio Tutela Vini Gambellara
Consorzio Tutela dei vini ad Origine Controllata Lison e Pramaggiore
Consorzio del Vino Prosecco dei Colli di Conegliano-Valdobbiadene
Consorzio Volontario per la Tutela della D.O.C. dei vini Colli Euganei
Consorzio dei vini tipici del Piave
Consorzio tutela del Vino Bardolino
Consorzio Tutela vino Bianco di Custoza D.O.C.
Consorzio Volontario per la tutela dei vini Soave e Recioto di Soave
Consorzio Volontario per la tutela dei vini Valpolicella e Recioto della Valpolicella

Friuli-Venezia Giulia
Consorzio Volontario per la tutela dei vini a D.O.C. Grave del Friuli
Consorzio Tutela vini D.O.C. Aquileia
Consorzio Tutela dei vini D.O.C. Latisana
Consorzio Tutela Denominazione Origine dei vini Colli Orientali
  del Friuli
Consorzio per la Tutela delle D.O. dei vini dell'Isonzo
Consorzio per la Tutela delle D.O. dei Vini del Collio
Consorzio per la difesa dei vini tipici e pregiati del Friuli

Emilia-Romagna
Consorzio Tutela Lambrusco Reggiano
Consorzio Tutela del Lambrusco
Consorzio per la Tutela del Gutturnio dei Colli Piacentini a D.O.C.
Consorzio di Tutela e valorizzazione del vino Lambrusco di Parma
Ente Tutela Vini Romagnoli a D.O.C.
Consorzio Volontario per la Tutela dei vini del comprensorio di
  Monte S. Pietro

Tuscany
Federazione Consorzi Vini Chianti
Consorzio del vino Chianti Putto
Consorzio Produttori Vino Chianti
Consorzio del vino Chianti
Consorzio Chianti Classico
Consorzio Chianti Centauro (Chianti e Chianti dell Colline Pisane)
Ente Tutela vini tipici di Empoli e della Val d'Elsa
Consorzio del vino Chianti Colli Empolesi
Consorzio per la tutela del vino Bianco dell'Empolese
Consorzio per la tutela della D.O. del vino Bianco Vergine Valdichiana
Consorzio del vino Rosso delle Colline Lucchesi a D.O.C.
Consorzio del vino Nobile di Montepulciano
Consorzio del vino Montecarlo Bianco
Consorzio del Vino Brunello di Montalcino
Consorzio del vino Bianco Pisano San Torpe D.O.C.
Consorzio Vino Candia
Consorzio vino D.O.C. Bianco di Pitigliano
Consorzio vino Vernaccia di San Gimignano
Consorzio vino Parrina Bianco e Rosso
Consorzio vini D.O.C. Elba Bianco ed Elba Rosso

Umbria and Lazio
Consorzio vino Orvieto Classico

Consorzio vini Alta Valle del Tevere
Consorzio Tutela Denominazione Frascati

Marche
Consorzio Volontario Tutela vini D.O.C. Rosso Piceno e Rosso
  Piceno Superiore
Consorzio per la difesa del vino tipico Rosso Conero
Consorzio per la difesa del Verdicchio dei Castelli di Jesi
Consorzio Volontario per la difesa del vino D.O.C. Bianchello del
  Metauro
Consorzio Volontario per la difesa del vino a D.O.C. Sangiovese dei
  Colli Pesaresi

Campania
Consorzio Vini Campani

Calabria
Consorzio Produttori Calabresi
Consorzio per la difesa dei vini tipici Cirò e Cirò Classico

Apulia
Consorzio per la Tutela del vino San Severo

Sicily
Consorzio Volontario per la Tutela del vino Marsala

Appendix 3

Select Bibliography

(a) The History of Wine in Italy

ALLEN, H. Warner, *A History of Wine*, London, 1961.
HENDERSON, Alexander, *The History of Ancient and Modern Wines*, London, 1824.
HYAMS, Edward, *Dionysus: A Social History of the Wine Vine*, London, 1965.
PENZER, N.M, *The Book of the Wine-Label*, London, 1947.
REDDING, Cyrus, *A History and Description of Modern Wines*, London, 1833 (third edition, with additions and corrections, 1860, consulted for this present work).
SELTMAN, Charles, *Wine in the Ancient World*, London, 1957.
SIMON, André, *The History of the Wine Trade in England*, London, 1905-6.
YOUNGER, William, *Gods, Men and Wine*, London, 1966.

(b) Italy, The Italians, Their Way of Life

BARZINI, Luigi, *The Italians*, London, 1964.
BONI, Ada, *Italian Regional Cooking*, London, 1969.
CHAMBERLAIN, Samuel, *Italian Bouquet*, New York, 1958.
DAVID, Elizabeth, *Italian Food*, London, 1964.

NICHOLS, Peter, *Italia, Italia*, London, 1973.
WALL, Bernard, *Italian Life and Landscape*, 2 vols., London, 1950.

(c) Works of Reference, Italian

BRUNI, Bruno, *Vini Italiani*, Bologna, 1964.
CAPONE, Roberto, *Vini Tipici e Pregiati d'Italia*, Florence, 1963.
CORIA, Giuseppe, *Enciclopedia dei Vini Italiani*, Verona, 1973.
MINISTERO DELL' AGRICOLTURA, *Principali Vitigni da Vino Colti-
vati in Italia*, 5 vols., Rome, 1952-66.
*PARONETTO, Lamberto (ed.), *Guida ai Vini d'Italia*, Milan, 1980.
VERONELLI, Luigi, *I Vini d'Italia*, Rome, 1961. (The edition in
English, published in Italy in 1964, is much abridged, and not
to be recommended.)

(d) Works of Reference, English

HOGG, Anthony, *Guide to Visiting Vineyards*, revised edition,
London, 1981.
JOHNSON, Hugh, *The World Atlas of Wine*, London, 1971.
LICHINE, Alexis, *Encyclopedia of Wines and Spirits*, revised edition,
London, 1979.
PEPPERCORN, David, and others, *Drinking Wine*, London, 1979.
PRICE, Pamela Vandyke, *The Taste of Wine*, London, 1975.
RONCARATI, Bruno, *Viva Vino*, London, 1978.

(e) General, Italian

CÙNSOLO, Felice, *Dizionario del Gourmet*, Milan, 1961.
MONELLI, Paolo, *O.P. Ossia il Vero Bevitore*, Milan, 1963.

(f) General, English

My own
RAY, Cyril, *The Wines of Italy*, London, 1966, was completely
superseded by
DALLAS, Philip, *Italian Wines*, London, 1974.

Things have moved so fast in Italy since then, thanks to the Italian

---

* The most up-to-date, comprehensive work of reference, giving the official
requirements for all D.O.C. wines, with chapters on the wine law (by Paolo Desana,
its moving spirit) and Italian viticulture, and much background information.

wine law, E.E.C. legislation, the growth of the co-operative movement, and much else – as I hope has been made clear in the
foregoing pages – that Mr Dallas then superseded himself with his
drily detailed, all too short, chapter in

SUTCLIFFE, Serena (ed.), *Wines of the World*, London, 1981.

Had Mr Dallas been given a book to write, rather than a chapter,
we might well have seen a book by an Englishman long resident in
Italy to match the long, far-ranging, idiosyncratic, detailed and
descriptive book by an American long resident in Italy:

ANDERSON, Burton, *Vino*, Boston, 1980.

Until Mr Anderson is superseded in his turn, this is far and away
the best book in English on Italian wines. I have learned an immense
amount from it, and have tried hard not to quarry from it more
material for my own considerably smaller and less ambitious book
– which is more a work of reference – than would seem reasonable.
What I have used I have acknowledged, and I hereby acknowledge
not only these borrowings but my own pleasure simply in reading
and dipping.

Appendix 4

Glossary

abboccato	slightly sweet
acerbo	sharp, tart
alcoolico	alcoholic
all'annata	of the year, referring to a young wine to be drunk the year after the vintage
amabile	sweeter than *abboccato*
amaro	bitter or very dry
amarognolo	very slightly bitter, but pleasantly so
annata	the year of the vintage
armonico	harmonious – a well-balanced wine
asciutto	completely dry, having been fully fermented out
autoclave	system used to making sparkling wine, in a tank, rather than by the champagne method (in French, *Charmat* and *cuve close*)
bianco	white
brillante	star-bright
cannellino	the sweet wines of the *castelli Romani* are so described for their cinnamon-like sweetness
cantina	cellar; winery
cantina sociale (co-operative)	a winery run by a co-operative of growers
casa vinicola	wine company
cerasuolo	cherry red, rosé
Charmat	see under *autoclave* (above)
chiaretto	very pale red
chinato	flavoured with quinine
classico	from the heart and the best part of the area
consorzio	a growers' association
corposo	with good body
cotto	cooked – a concentrated wine
D.O.C.	*Denominazione di Origine Controllata*
D.O.C.G.	*Denominazione di Origine Controllata e Garantita*
D.O.S.	*Denominazione di Origine Semplice* (no longer applicable)
delicato	delicate
dolce	richly sweet
etereo	ethereal: sometimes applied to a wine's bouquet
fattoria	farm: hence, frequently, wine-growing property, estate

fiasco	flask
frizzante	semi-sparkling, equivalent of *pétillant*; not so fizzy as *spumante*
fruttato	fruity
Gay Lussac	measure of alcohol by volume
generoso	generous, a warm, full-bodied wine
giallo paglierino	straw yellow – the pale colour of many dry white wines
gradi (gradi alcoolico)	alcoholic strength; percentage of alcohol by volume
imbottigliato	bottled
alla fattoria	at the winery
del prodottore all' origine	at the estate
in zona d'origine	in the growing area
nell' origine	at the estate
nello stabili- mento della ditta	at the premises of the company
infiascato	put in flasks (see above)
limpido	limpid; when a wine is clear
liquoroso	adjective applied to a sweet wine of high alcoholic degree, often fortified with alcohol
invecchiato	aged
maderizzato	maderized; oxidized by reason of age or exposure to air. Gives white wines brownish tint and taste
Mezzogiorno	southern Italy, including Sicily and Sardinia
morbido	soft
muffa nobile	noble rot; the botrytis that attacks certain grapes from which luscious dessert wines are then made. French: *pourriture noble*; German: *Edelfaule*
mussante	sparkling
nero	black; used for deep red wines
ossidato	same as *maderizzato* (above)
passito	semi-dried – referring to grapes used to make sweet wine and to the wine itself
pastoso	mouth-filling
pieno	full
profumato	perfumed
recioto amarone	a wine made from grapes that have been dried to concentrate their juice
retrogusto	after-taste
riserva	a wine aged for a statutory period according to legislation and tradition
gran riserva (and riserva speciale)	wine aged for an even longer period
rosato	rosé, pink
rosso	red
rosso granato	garnet red
rosso rubino	ruby red
rotondo	round

sapido	with a lively taste
scelto	selected
secco	dry
spumante	frothy, hence sparkling
stoffa	when a wine is rich, deep and complex, it is sometimes said to have 'stuff'
stravecchio	very old
superiore	a wine made from selected grapes, usually matured in wood for a year or so longer
tannico	tannic
tappo	cork
tenementi	holding or estate
vecchio	old
vellutato	velvety
vendemmia	vintage
vino da taglio	cutting wine; a wine (frequently from the south) with high alcohol content and deep colour (for reds) added to (usually more northern) wines to give them more body
vino da tavola	table wine
vinoso	vinous
V.Q.P.R.D.	*Vin de Qualité Produit en Région Déterminée*; an E.E.C. classification for all quality wines produced in a specific area – i.e. D.O.C. and D.O.C.G. wines in Italy
zuccheraggio	*chaptalisation*; the addition of sugar which then ferments into greater alcoholic strength

Index

154

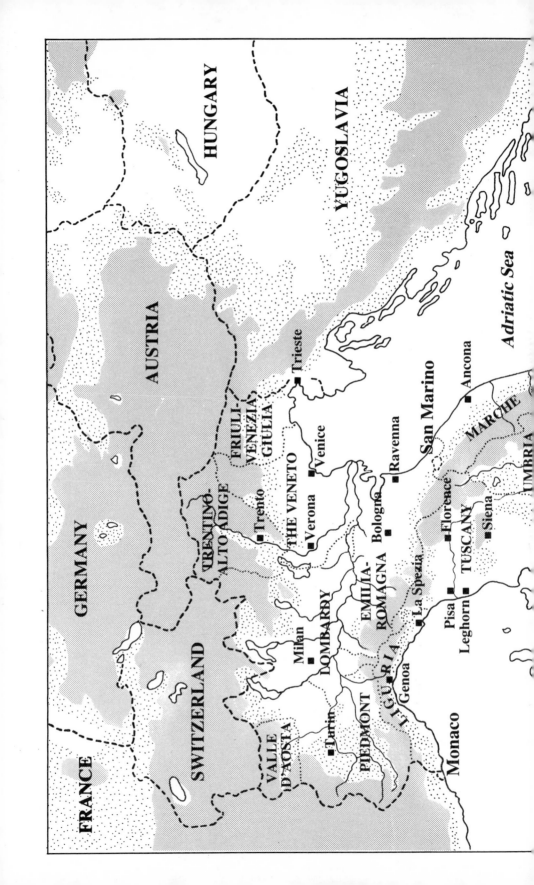